I. INTRODUCTION

A. MAJOR RESEARCH QUESTION

South Korea has undergone many drastic transformations from the time when it formally emerged as a state in 1948 until now, becoming a thriving democracy and the world's 12th-largest economy.[1] Three generations of Korean women, starting with my grandmother's, have lived through different stages of this change. I recall my grandmother's unfathomable tales of what it was like to live under the Japanese occupation and what the country endured in the aftermath of the Korean War—starvation, poverty, and confusion. My mother's stories of a few decades later describe another generation's nightly curfews under the strict military rule of President Park Chung-Hee, combined with the rise of economic prosperity, when more and more Koreans could enjoy modern amenities like refrigerators, televisions, cars, and denim jeans. Still, I also remember my mother's story of how neighbors in her quiet fishing town in the mid-1970s condemned her entire family when she attended a university. The neighbors could not comprehend money being "wasted" on a mere girl. More traditional viewpoints about women's place in society held firm amid burgeoning prosperity, even as the country embarked on democratization.

On the one hand, women in South Korea have enjoyed many aspects of the country's recovery and rise. According to the 2013 World Economic Forum's Annual Gender Gap Index, South Korean women today have the highest literacy and healthy life expectancy rates in the world.[2] On the other hand, according to the same index, South Korea ranked at 111 out of 136 countries in gender equality.[3] Moreover, South Korea ranked the worst overall when compared to all other countries in the East Asian region: the Philippines ranked fifth in the world; China, 69th place; and Japan, 105th.[4] Notably, South Korea's gender equality is weakest on the

---

[1] "The World Factbook: South Korea," Central Intelligence Agency, accessed 24 March 2015, https://www.cia.gov/library/publications/the-world-factbook/geos/ks.html.

[2] Ricardo Hausmann, Saadia Zahidi, Laura Tyson, Klaus Schwab, and Laura D'Andrea Tyson, "Global Gender Gap Report 2013," The World Economic Forum, assessed on 20 May 2014, http://reports.weforum.org/global-gender-gap-report-2013.

[3] Ibid.

[4] Hausmann et al., "Global Gender Gap Report 2013," 244.

subindex for political empowerment.[5] The statistics seem to show real boundaries to South Korea's democratic progress, at least for its women.

Although this index highlights the need for improvement, the ranking does not illustrate how far Korea has progressed from my grandmother's era to the present, especially considering that the country has recently elected its first female president, Park Geun-hye. Most studies tend to overlook political indicators for women: they focus on a handful of other data points that can be more easily compared between countries. In addition, these data are static, representing a short period – a snapshot in time. Another problem is that the indices focus on particular sub-indicators that do not necessarily present a complete picture of women's empowerment. Despite its low ranking when compared to the rest of the world, South Korea is making true progress that is likely to continue, particularly in the area of politics. There is more to this story than the indices show, and additional factors can more fully depict South Korea's progress toward greater empowerment for women.

Static measurement cannot completely illustrate the changing status of Korea's women. Progress is a critical element. This paper does not argue that South Korea is improperly ranked in gender equality when compared globally. Rather, it seeks to show that in measuring and predicting future growth in political empowerment, change over time can demonstrate progress. By analyzing current criteria used in empowerment measurements for women and determining which indicators should matter specifically to women at all levels within a society, this thesis illustrates how the current gauges are not enough to accurately measure progress. I argue that South Korea's empowerment progress over time is of primary importance, considering its low starting point and significant challenges to overcome. I will examine the power of the women's movement, women's successful gain of seats in parliament, and policies enacted toward significant improvements in women's status to give a more complete picture of women's political empowerment in South Korea.

B. SIGNIFICANCE OF THE RESEARCH QUESTION

According to South Korea's 2013 government data, a more naturally expected sex ratio at birth has helped propel the female population to represent almost exactly half of the entire

---

[5] Hausmann et al., "Gender Gap Report 2013," 244.

population, with 25.08 million women versus 25.14 million men.[6] If women make up half the population, their representation in the country's policy and decision-making should be proportional in a gender-equal society. The Global Gender Gap Index, established in 2006 by the World Economic Forum, "addresses the need for consistent and comprehensive measure of gender equality that can track a country's progress over time."[7] As such, the Global Gender Gap Report examines areas of inequality between men and women in 136 countries, and focuses on economic participation and opportunity, political empowerment, educational attainment, and health-based criteria.

While accounts of gender inequality and the lack of women's political power and representation are widely available, methodological approaches designed specifically to measure the nation's progress for women are rare. For example, current methods often fail to capture phenomena that affect national and local governmental policies: the Global Gender Gap Index Report highlights in its report "a clear drawback in [the political empowerment category due to] the absence of any indicators capturing differences between the participation of women and men at local levels of government."[8]

A more complete analysis might better capture progress from the past to the present using not only standard-issue indicators, but also more qualitative measures of the momentum of the women's movement and the emergence of such tangible responses to society's actual demands for greater women's empowerment as changes in institutions and policies. Accurate measures of empowerment can thus help identify deficiencies and develop policies to correct them. This research will analyze current criteria used and suggest indicators that illustrate a fuller picture.

C. LITERATURE REVIEW

A small number of concepts and measurements are currently accepted and used by international organizations to measure gender equality and development. According to scholars in gender equality, "To date, there have been relatively few attempts to provide the means of

---

[6] In-Soo Nam, "South Korean Women Get Even, At Least in Number," *Wall Street Journal* (blog), 1 July 2013, http://blogs.wsj.com/korearealtime/2013/07/01/south-korean-females-get-even-at-least-in-number/.

[7] Hausmann et al., "Global Gender Gap 2013," 3.

[8] Ibid., 4.

assessing whether policy interventions are having an empowering effect."[9] The GGI and GII indices come closest to serving as acceptable methods for explaining inequality and charting disparities between men and women in important categories. However, these measurements fall short when measuring advancement and empowerment. Political movements are essential to understanding the progress of Korean women's empowerment and to measuring development.

Although this paper will touch on different aspects of women's participation within the society, it will focus mainly on the elements that lead to women's political empowerment. Evidence suggests that women press for different political priorities than those emphasized by men: they are "more active in supporting laws benefiting women, children, and families."[10] Women's political participation supports fair representation of women's interest in the decision-making process. Further, "evidence suggests that women's participation in political decision-making bodies improves the quality of governance."[11] Notably, studies have found a positive correlation between increased women's participation in public life and a reduction in the level of corruption.[12] As such, understanding women's political progress improves South Korea's government and its policies.

1. **Political Empowerment**

Fundamentally, in order to understand theories about women's empowerment, the first step is to define "power" and "empowerment." According to feminist scholars, "individual and collective participation … [is] an important foundational concept for analyzing empowerment."[13] *Power* within the term "women's empowerment," is "fluid, relational and connected to control over discourse and knowledge."[14] Bookman and Morgen use the term empowerment "to connote

---

[9] Ruth Alsop, Mette Bertelsen, and Jeremy Holland, *Empowerment in Practice: From Analysis to Implementation* (Washington, DC: The World Bank, 2006), 30.

[10] Caren Grown, Geeta Rao Gupta, and Aslihan Kes, *Taking Action: Achieving Gender Equality and Empowering Women* (London: Earthscan, 2005), 104.

[11] Grown et al., *Taking Action: Achieving Gender Equality and Empowering Women*, 104–10.

[12] Ibid., 105.

[13] Jane L. Parpart, Shirin M. Rai, and Kathleen A. Staudt, eds. *Rethinking Empowerment: Gender and Development in a Global/Local World*, (London: Routledge, 2003), 7.

[14] Ibid., 7–8.

a spectrum of political activity ranging from acts of individual resistance to mass political mobilizations that challenge the basic power relations in our society."[15]

Many studies have defined women's power in various forms; many experts agree power derives from participation in the events and processes that shape their lives.[16] The United Nations Development Programme (UNDP) Human Development Report identifies four basic forms of participation: household, economic, social and cultural, and political.[17] These "participations are an essential element of human development," and when women achieve access in decision-making and the power of direct or indirect control over the processes that affect their lives, the result should be a society more responsive to the needs of all people.[18] As argued by Karl, "In bringing new insights and contributions to all issues, [such empowerment] will enrich and shift the focus and content of discourse in politics and society to include a wider range of views."[19]

Call it growth. Empowerment is defined as a group's or individual's ability to make competent decisions, "that is, to make choices and then to transform those choices into desired actions and outcomes."[20] As such, analysts are better served by conceiving of "power that recognizes the importance of individual consciousness and understanding [and the] importance of collective action … that can organize and exert power to challenge hierarchies and improve women's lives."[21] Bookman and Morgen note, "Empowerment begins when they change their ideas about the causes of their powerlessness, when they recognize the systemic forces that oppress them, and when they act to change the condition of their lives."[22] Hence, the focus must be on institutional structures and politics, and acknowledgement that empowerment is both a

---

[15] Ann Bookman and Sandra Morgen, *Women and the Politics of Empowerment,* (Philadelphia: Temple University Press, 1988), 4.

[16] Marilee Karl, *Women and Empowerment: Participation and Decision Making,* Vol. 10 (London: Zed Books, 1995), 2.

[17] Ibid.

[18] Ibid.

[19] Ibid., 1.

[20] Alsop et al., *Empowerment in Practice: From Analysis to Implementation,* 10.

[21] Parpart et al., *Rethinking Empowerment: Gender and Development in a Global/Local World,* 7–8.

[22] Bookman and Morgen, *Women and the Politics of Empowerment,* 4.

process and an outcome.[23] Women's empowerment through political participation can be gained through various avenues, such as "electoral politics, public life, or non-governmental organizations, and movements."[24]

The term political life encompasses attempts to manipulate power via voting, lobbying, or even running for elective office.[25] Additionally, it includes those that turn their attention to politics only when they feel their interests are directly threatened.[26] Thus, political empowerment is "analyzed in global and national as well as local terms."[27]

Tuminez and Desai argue, "While development has benefitted women, the relationship between human development and female leadership is not directly proportional."[28] It is the government and institutions that directly seize opportunities and remove barriers, allowing women to progress in politics. Furthermore, as argued by Jones, "the political structures of democratization have enabled women and their allies to not only sustain their mobilization efforts over time, but to also secure significant policy, institutional, and representational change."[29]

Htun adds, "As the twentieth century progressed, a consensus emerged in international society and within democratic polities that one social segment should not monopolize political power."[30] Accordingly, women's empowerment helps explain changes in social, cultural, and political systems.[31] The political growth of Korean women was moved along by organizations that capitalized on and exercised influence on political decision-making and mobilized public

---

[23] Parpart et al., *Rethinking Empowerment: Gender and Development in a Global/Local World*, 3–4.

[24] Karl, *Women and Empowerment: Participation and Decision Making*, 14.

[25] Bookman and Morgen, *Women and the Politics of Empowerment*, 298.

[26] Ibid.

[27] Ibid.

[28] Astrid S. Tuminez and Vishakha N. Desai, "Power to Women in Asia: It's Time to Remove the Entrenched Social and Cultural Barriers that Prevent Women from Fulfilling Their Potential," *Straight Times*, 19 May 2012, http://newshub.nus.edu.sg/news/1205/PDF/POWER-st-19may-pD12.pdf.

[29] Nicola Anne Jones, *Gender and the Political Opportunities of Democratization in South Korea*, (Gordonsville, VA : Macmillan 2006), 2.

[30] Mala Htun, "Is Gender Like Ethnicity? Political Representation of Identity Groups," *Perspectives on Politics* 2, no. 03 (2004), 439.

[31] Doonwon Suh, "The Dual Strategy and Gender Policies of the Women's Movement in Korea: Family Headship System in Repeal through Strategic Innovation," *Sociological Focus* 44, no. 2 (2011), 125–126.

opinion on women's issues.[32] Lee argues, "If civil society provides a potential field for political empowerment of women in new democracies, women's organizations are key players in civil society."[33] Specifically, South Korea's progress in gender relations has been aided by the inter-related implementation of policies and laws, increases in the role of the women's movement, and women's gains in political representation.

2. Societal, Structural, and International Influence

Changing economic realities have been the driving force behind women's empowerment. Democratic institutions and policies have then supported growth, incorporating women's interests and advancements. This engine of economics and politics is transforming an andocentric society into a more egalitarian one. By enforcing the development of women's empowerment, economics and politics are then changing culture and civil society. Additionally, external pressures have contributed to these changes. The international community's influence has help guide South Korea's internal political dialogue over increasing women's political status.

The South Korean case is a good example of how women's advancement can result in part from changes in structural and institutional factors. For instance, the Korean *hoju* system, a family registration system under civil law dating back to 1953, was abolished on January 1, 2008 " after the Constitutional Court had announced (in 2005) that it was incompatible with the constitution.[34] For scholars in women's studies, the *hoju* system represented "an outdated patriarchy informed by Confucianism," since the system required that "daughters become members of their husband's family's when they marry, and women only inherit the position of family head when there are no surviving males."[35] Conservatives contended that "gender hierarchy in the family [is] a core value of the Korean culture and therefore argued to preserve it."[36] Though controversial, the abolition of the system helped Korea move toward a more

---

[32] Aie-Rie Lee & Hyun-Chool Lee, "The Women's Movement in South Korea Revisited," *Asian Affairs: An American Review* 40, no. 2 (2013), 44.

[33] Ibid., 64.

[34] Eunkang Koh, "Gender issues and Confucian scriptures: Is Confucianism incompatible with gender equality in South Korea?," *Bulletin of the School of Oriental and African Studies* 71, no. 02 (2008), 346.

[35] Ibid.

[36] Ki-young Shin, "The Politics of the Family Law Reform Movement in Contemporary Korea: A Contentious Space for Gender and the Nation," *Journal of Korean Studies* 11, no. 1 (Fall 2006), 93.

gender-equal society and was "the result of cooperation between government, especially the Ministry of Gender Equality and Family, and non-governmental organizations such as Korea Women's Associations United."[37] According to Koh, "many people, not just those who identify themselves as 'feminists' joined the movement to abolish the *hoju* system ... as they agreed that the *hoju* system should be abolished in order to promote gender equality and the dignity of the individual."[38]

Another example of institutional change is the government's expansion of its family policies. Under conservative governments in South Korea from 1988 to 1997, "family policy did not receive much attention."[39] Later, though, "the election of the center-left government advanced the political weight of feminist women's groups," and the principal center-left party "adopted [a] progressive agenda including family policy into the election manifesto and spearheaded the expansion" of programs such as tax-funded maternity and paternity leave schemes, increased paid maternity leave time, and child care benefits.[40] Most recently, through its National Childcare Strategy, "the government pledged doubling the number of child care centers and introduced different child care benefits, [including] the so-called 'basic subsidy' (covering half of the private child care costs of every child younger than the age of 2)."[41] Policy changes in Korea have pushed the rise in Korean women's status and progress toward empowerment.

Additionally, such changes signify a shift away from Korean Confucian family values and ideas of women's primary role as childcare provider, toward a more equal role between men and women. Cultural changes in Korea are occurring. Changes such as Korean women's socioeconomic status have played a significant role in critically evaluating the previously-existing cultural and political system. According to scholars, "Women's formal political

---

[37] Shin, "The Politics of the Family Law Reform Movement in Contemporary Korea," 93.

[38] Koh, "Gender issues and Confucian scriptures: Is Confucianism incompatible with gender equality in South Korea?," *Bulletin of the School of Oriental and African Studies* 71, no. 02 (2008), 346.

[39] Timo Fleckenstein and Soohyun Christine Lee, "The Politics of Postindustrial Social Policy Family Policy Reforms in Britain, Germany, South Korea, and Sweden," Comparative Political Studies 47, no. 4 (2014), 619.

[40] Ibid., 619–620.

[41] Ibid., 620.

participation and empowerment is built on the precursors of education and economic opportunities."[42]

Mobilization to press for the political fruits of such cultural change is also crucial. Mobilization of the women's movement during South Korea's rapid industrialization and economic development, and the interaction of this movement with the newly democratized South Korean state, allowed women to achieve tangible progress in the form of political outcomes. As generational shift has narrowed the gender gap, citizens—including but not limited to women—are exhibiting "growing interest…in political and economic reforms and other societal issues [that] coincided with [the government's] need to support from civil society in advocating its political and public policy agendas."[43]

Furthermore, international influence has increased opportunities for Korean women to pursue greater political representation. The United Nations' Committee on the Elimination of Discrimination against Women (CEDAW) is "used in advocating for women's equal political participation in Asia-Pacific both by transnational networks of gender advocates, government and non-government actors."[44] As a part of the global movement for gender equity, they have sanctioned the international "women's bill of rights."[45] Along with Korean women's capitalizing on the external organizational pressures, they were able to help guide institutional mechanisms to meet the needs of its citizens.[46]

3. Conventional Methods' Shortcomings

Conventional methods such as GGI and GII used by international organizations inadequately measure progress. Measurement of gender equality gaps at the country-to-country lack specific details on the trajectory of a country's internal change with respect to gender political representation and participation. Good measures should be able to answer basic

---

[42] Jacqui True, Sara Niner, Swati Parashar, and Nicole George, "2012 Women's Political Participation in Asia and the Pacific." In *New York: SSRC Conflict Prevention and Peace Forum,* 14.

[43] Eui Hang Shin, "The Role of NGOs in Political Elections in South Korea: The Case of Citizens' Alliance for the 2000 General Election," *Asian Survey* 43, no. 4 (July/August 2003), 697.

[44] Jacqui True et al., "2012 Women's Political Participation in Asia and the Pacific," 6.

[45] Ibid.

[46] Ibid.

questions such as who, what, why, and how. Conventional gender equality indices do not provide sufficient perspective on exactly "who" is the subject matter, because they are unable to incorporate the importance of culture and how widely cultures can vary across the world. The indices also fail to answer "why" gender equality variances occur, because they do not fully consider barriers and limitations of specific countries.

Cultures of different regions and countries differ widely. Results derived from a global index measurement cannot capture all cultural variances, and depict a less than full picture of actual gender status. South Korea has witnessed a profound transformation in its civil society and will continue to transform. Although more than 60 years have passed since South Korea's establishment and adoption of the Constitution, its democratic government is still relatively young and changes are still ongoing. One reason for the slow progress in equality is Confucianism. Soh defines the Confucianism entrenched in Korean society: "The concept of sexual equality, in fact, is fundamentally alien to the Confucian worldview, which regards society as an 'ordered inequality'…helping to reinforce the inequalities in social status based on gender, age, and social positions."[47] Korea has preserved Confucianism and a patriarchal system of gender relations for over two thousand years of recorded history.[48] To eliminate the entrenched cultural gender disparity, Chin posits, "The state must actively effect radical changes in the social, economic, educational, legal, and political fields."[49]

Furthermore, conventional measurements provide unclear explanation as to "how" the data should be interpreted because they do not provide solutions that are targeted to specific countries' situations. South Korean scores on these indices may portray below-average standards, but considering the country's heavily patriarchal culture, the scores might actually not be as deficient. According to Inchoon Kim, "The women's movement in Korea has been the most important factor in bringing about changes in gender politics."[50] Moreover, these women's

---

[47] Soh, Chung-Hee Sarah. "Sexual Equality, Male Superiority, and Korean Women in Politics: Changing Gender Relations in a "patriarchal Democracy."" Sex Roles 28, no. 1–2 (1993): 74.

[48] Sirin Sung, "Women reconciling paid and unpaid work in a Confucian welfare state: The case of South Korea," *Social policy & administration* 37, no. 4 (2003): 346.

[49] Mikyung Chin, "Reflections on Women's Empowerment through Local Representation in South Korea," *Asian Survey* 44, no. 2 (2004): 296.

[50] Inchoon Kim, "Developments and Characteristics of Gender Politics in South Korea: A Comparative Perspective," *Korea Observer* 43, no 4 (Winter 2012), 558,

actions sought involvement through institutions, adopted new institutions and policies, and fostered a positive view toward women.

4. Global Gender Gap and Gender Inequality Indexes

The World Economic Forum's Global Gender Gap Index "benchmarks national gender gaps on economic, political, education and health criteria, and provides country rankings that allow for effective comparisons across regions and income groups, over time."[51] The country rankings create global audience awareness of challenges concerning gender inequality.[52] The Global Gender Gap Index explores and analyzes the gap between men and women in four principal categories: "Economic Participation and Opportunity, Educational Attainment, Health and Survival, and Political Empowerment."[53]

The category of Economic Participation and Opportunity incorporates the following three sub-index gaps: participation, remuneration, and advancement.[54] The participation gap highlights the imbalance in labor force participation rates; the remuneration gap focuses on variation in female-to-male earned income and "a qualitative variable calculated through the World Economic Forum's Executive Opinion Survey (wage equality for similar work)."[55] Last in this sub-index, the advancement category illustrates—using hard-data statistics—gaps in advancement via the ratio of women to men among legislators, senior officials, and managers, and the ratio of women to men among technical and professional workers.

The Educational Attainment category measures the gap between women's and men's access to primary, secondary, and tertiary-level education. The third category, Health and Survival, "provides [an] overview of the differences between women's and men's health."[56] Last, the Political Empowerment category measures the gap between men and women at "the highest level of political decision-making, through the ratio of women to men in parliamentary positions," and the divergence between men and women in "terms of years in executive office

---

[51] Hausmann et al., "Global Gender Gap Report 2013," 3.
[52] Ibid.
[53] Ibid., 4.
[54] Ibid.
[55] Ibid.
[56] Ibid.

(prime minister or president)."[57] In Korea, women's changing socioeconomic status and societal attitudes are slowly beginning to lessen the gap, and women's political contributions are gaining importance. Korean women have come to occupy prestigious positions in government, from the presidency and prime ministership to the chairs of political parties and of Legislature policy committees, not to mention rank-and-file legislators' positions. Thus, an argument can be made that not only has the quantity of Korean women's political participation increased, but also that this participation has been achieved at a high level of quality and influence as well.

Much the same as the World Economic Forum's Gender Gap Report, the United Nations Human Development Report's Global Inequality Index (GII) reflects gender-based inequalities in three dimensions—reproductive health, empowerment, and economic activity. Reproductive health is measured by maternal mortality and adolescent birth rates; empowerment is measured by the share of parliamentary seats held by women and attainment in secondary and higher education by each gender; and economic activity is measured by the labor market participation rate for women and men. "The GII for 149 countries reveal the extent to which national achievements in reproductive health, empowerment and labor markets participation are eroded by gender inequality."[58] In turn, the study's conclusions help illustrate the degree to which women can take an active part in economic and political matters.[59]

Table 1.   Measurement of Political Empowerment[60]

Global Gender Gap Report	Gender Inequality Index
Women in Parliament	Shared Seats in Parliament (% held by women)
Women in Ministerial Positions	Population with at least some secondary education (% ages 25 and older)
Years with Female Head of State (last 50)	

Despite their use of similar categories and indicators, the two reports introduced above differ significantly in how they rank different countries' degree of gender inequality. For

---

[57] Hausmann et al., "Gender Gap Report 2013," 4.

[58] Ibid., 39.

[59] Alsop et al., *Empowerment in Practice: From Analysis to Implementation*, 229–230.

[60] Created chart using the 2013 Gender Gap Report and 2013 Gender Inequality Index.

example, the measurement of political empowerment in GII includes only two factors—attainment of secondary and higher education by each gender from age 25 and up, and percent of parliamentary seats held by women. On the other hand, the Gender Gap Report used measurements as explained previously. Moreover, the two indices are based on different analytical aims and have different explanations. The different methodologies, as demonstrated by the political empowerment category in the respective reports, help explain the divergent outcomes in the overall ranking.

In addition, the current conventional measurements are more focused on inequality and gender gaps, and less focused on empowerment. The concept of empowerment is correlated to gender equality but the two terms hold distinctive meanings. The Oxford English Dictionary defines "gap" as "a difference, especially an undesirable one, between two views or situations."[61] As such, reports that depict gender gaps compare a factor and its difference between men and women. In contrast, "The core of empowerment lies in the ability of a woman to control her own destiny."[62] This implies that to be empowered women must not only have equal capabilities (such as education and health) and equal access to resources and opportunities (such as land and employment), but they must also have the agency to use those rights, capabilities, resources, and opportunities to make strategic choices and decisions (such as is provided through leadership opportunities and participation in political institutions).[63] The various uses of gender gaps as a proxy for gender inequality depict only specific points of time in measuring women's advancement, and cannot sufficiently take into account the factors outlined above. An index that can better capture the progress of women's empowerment, the momentum of the women's movement, and changes in institution and policies will be able to better accurately measure gender advancements.

5. Economic Participation and Opportunity

Historical examples abound of women's exclusion from the world of politics; South Korea is no exception. Confucian thought, which fails to hold women in esteem equal to men, has heavily

---

[61] Oxford English Dictionaries, Oxford University Press, accessed 25 September 2014, http://www.oxforddictionaries.com/us/definition/american_english/gap.

[62] Grown et al., *Taking Action: Achieving Gender Equality and Empowering Women*, 33.

[63] Ibid., 31–32.

influenced Korea. Although Confucian traditions strongly steered the peninsula toward becoming a male-dominated country, the status of women in today's society is changing due to the implementation of policies such as the Equal Employment Opportunity Act (1987) and the Gender Discrimination Prevention and Relief Act (1999), designed to bring equality between sexes.[64] In Korea, industrialization and urbanization transformed women's socioeconomic status dramatically, aiding their pursuit of social improvements and greater political representation. Increasing economic status, higher education, and strengthening social capital provided the conditions for Korean women to be more involved in civic life, and as a result, to make greater demand for equal representation in politics. The GGI data show women's empowerment, but one can see a clearer picture by viewing the same data chronologically. Table 2 depicts progress toward increased political empowerment using the GGI from 2006 to 2013.

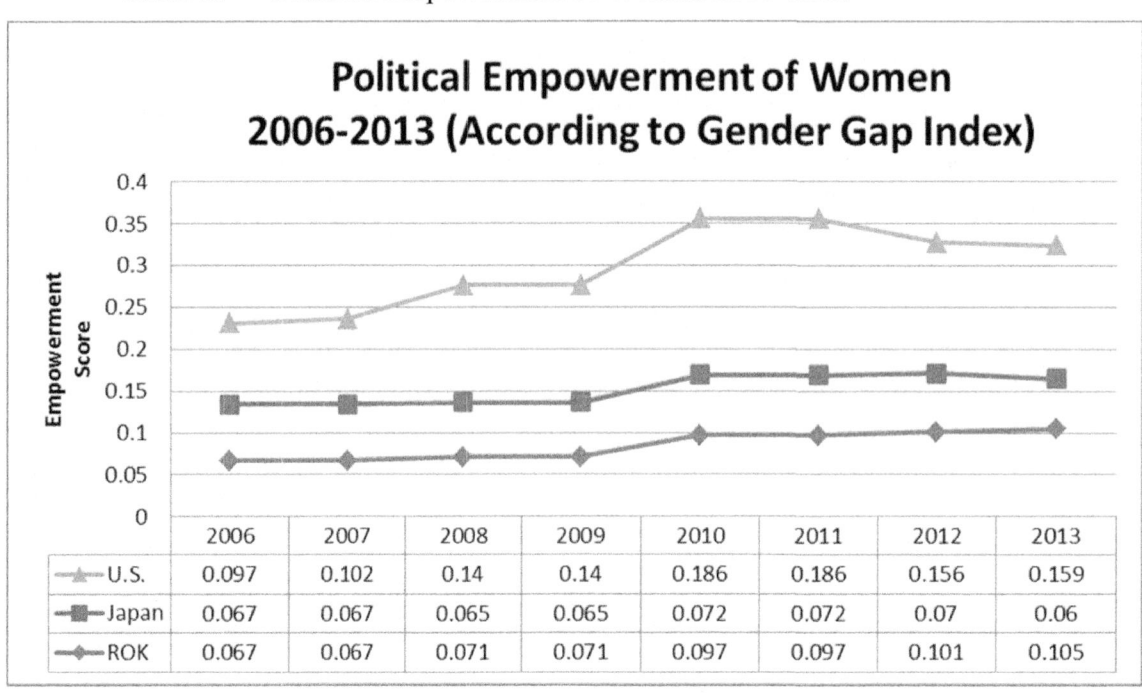

Table 2. Political Empowerment of Women 2006–2013[65]

Political Empowerment of Women 2006-2013 (According to Gender Gap Index)

	2006	2007	2008	2009	2010	2011	2012	2013
U.S.	0.097	0.102	0.14	0.14	0.186	0.186	0.156	0.159
Japan	0.067	0.067	0.065	0.065	0.072	0.072	0.07	0.06
ROK	0.067	0.067	0.071	0.071	0.097	0.097	0.101	0.105

---

[64] Jae-seon Joo, "Statistical Analysis of Changes in the Status of South Korean Women," GSPR 2013 Vol. 6, 168. http://eng.kwdi.re.kr/gspr/view.do?idx=8.

[65] Derived from Political Empowerment data in GGI for the respective countries from 2006–2013

Scholars from social, economic, and political science fields argue that gender equity can be measured in various approaches such as economic participation and opportunity. Matland notes that "countries with higher levels of GDP per capita and that had been more progressive in terms of defining the role of women in society tended to be more open to women."[66] Lee argues that Korea's economic boost led to circumstances in which "the full-fledged national movement for modernization required massive participation of a female workforce, and thus women became—perhaps unintentionally—major contributors to national development."[67] Henceforth, with economic freedom gained from employment and opportunities for higher education, the Korean women's movement and the pursuit of political power involved promising circumstances for identity formation and mobilization of gender status.

Although South Korea's economic development aided the progress of the women's movement, it did not directly lead to empowerment. The economic development did not resolve "many existing forms of women's subordination and introduced new forms of exploitation and oppression."[68] Wieringa expounds on the lack of correlation between the economic growth and improvement of gender development via Heyzer's investigation on "the performance of the development process in Asia and the Pacific in relations to women's issues."[69] Heyzer's main argument is that "high growth…is not a precondition for gender equity, as the *World Development Report* maintains, for 'gender equity may actually worsen under certain growth patterns.'"[70] High rates of economic growth do not necessarily correlate with benefits for women.[71] Figure 1 shows corresponding GDP per capita *vis-a-vis* the World Gender Gap Ranking Index and United Nations Human Development Report's GII.

---

[66] Richard E. Matland, "Structuring Representation: Women's Access to Political Power across the World," *Harvard International Review* 32, no. 1 (2010), 48.

[67] Aie-Rie Lee, "Consistency or Change in Women's Politicization in South Korea," *Policy Studies Journal* 24, no. 2 (1996), 183.

[68] Saskia Wieringa, "Women's Interests and Empowerment: Gender Planning Reconsidered," *Development and Change* 25, no. 4 (1994): 830.

[69] Ibid., 831.

[70] Ibid., 831.

[71] Ibid. 830.

GDP per capita vis-a-vis GII

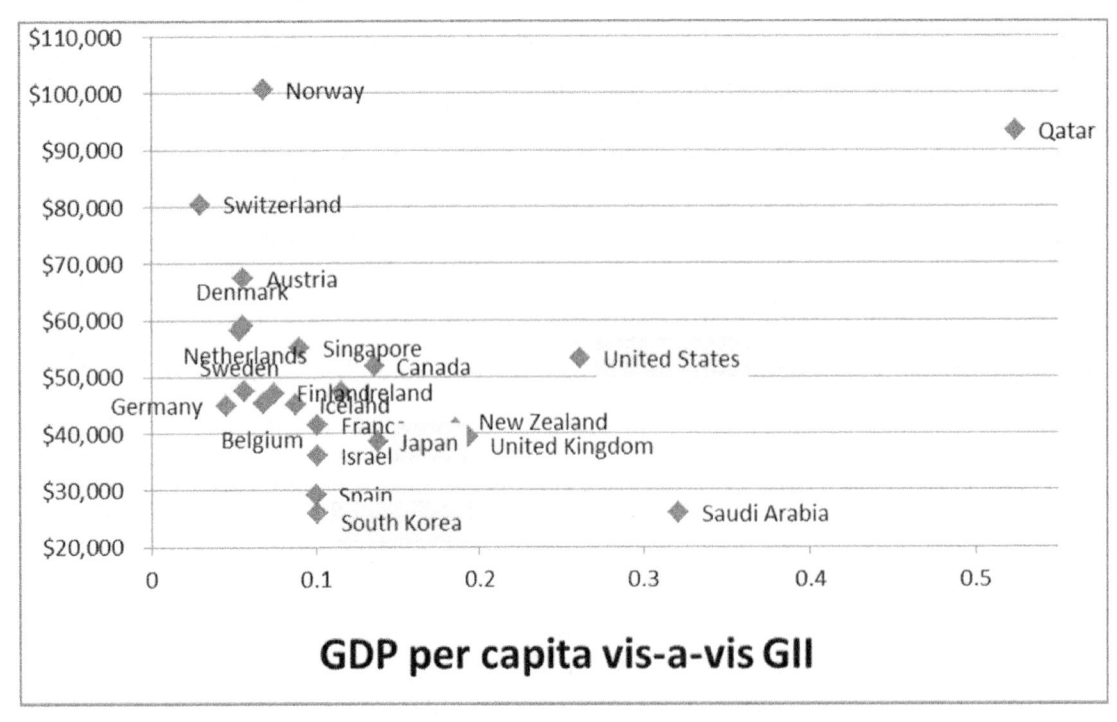

Figure 1.   GDP per Capita *vis-a-vis* GII[72]

The argument that GDP and social advancement through higher education and economic participation are correlated to gender equality and women's progress has validity. However, the factors provide more than a simple or linear measurement of women's empowerment. The rise in socioeconomic change led to change in social status and was a significant contributing factor for Korean women's status. It was one important element that aided this progress, but other contributing factors must also be considered to account for women's political empowerment. In addition, economic change does not completely explain why gender inequality still exists in high-income and developed states such as the United States, Japan, and South Korea. Table 3 lists these three countries' GDPs and their respective rankings in the World Gender Gap Ranking Index and United Nations Human Development Report's GII. Despite the same high levels of economic development and GDP, the different measures of equality result in wildly different rankings. This variance highlights the need for more a precise method of measuring gender equality and women's empowerment.

---

[72] Figure 1 was derived from comparing selective high income countries with the GDP per capita and GII index.

Table 3.   U.S., Japan, and ROK's GDP, Rankings in GGI and GII

Year	2013	2013	2013	2013	2013	2013
	World Gender Gap Index[73] Ranking (Out of 136 countries)	GII[74] Ranking (Out of 149 countries)	GDP[75] Dollar	Per Capita Income (PCI)[76] Dollar	Human Development Index (HDI)[77] Index	HDI[78] Rank
U.S.	31	47	$16.8 Trillion	$53,143	0.914	5
Japan	105	25	$4.9 Trillion	$38,492	0.890	17
ROK	111	17	$1.3 Trillion	$25,977	0.891	15

D. POTENTIAL EXPLANATIONS AND HYPOTHESES

While the conventional indices describe Korean women's political empowerment status as unfavorable, closer examination of similar factors beyond just numbers is necessary to understand the whole story. The divergence from conventional methods to measure real progress in women's political empowerment can be accomplished through both quantitative data and qualitative examination of progress, using not only the standard-issue indicators, but also attention to the momentum of the women's movement and the development of tangible means to meet society's actual demands through changes in institutions and policies.

I will focus on the progress over time of standard indicators, the momentum and power of the women's movement, and policies that make significant improvements in women's empowerment to explain women's political empowerment in South Korea. I will review progress

---

[73] Organizational Economic Cooperation and Development, accessed 10 August 2014. http://www.oecd.org/about/membersandpartners/list-oecd-member-countries.htm.

[74] Human Development Reports: Gender Inequality Index, United Nations Development Programme, accessed 19 August 2014, http://hdr.undp.org/en/content/table-4-gender-inequality-index.

[75] World Bank, Gross Domestic Product, accessed 10 August 2014. http://data.worldbank.org/indicator/NY.GDP.MKTP.CD.

[76] World Bank, Per Capita Income, accessed 10 August 2014. http://data.worldbank.org/indicator/NY.GDP.PCAP.CD.

[77] World Bank, Human Development Index, accessed 10 August 2014. http://hdr.undp.org/en/content/human-development-index-hdi.

[78] World Bank, Human Development Index, accessed 10 August 2014. http://hdr.undp.org/en/content/human-development-index-hdi.

in policy output, including current president Park Geun-hye's domestic policies and changes to the Ministry of Gender Equality, as well as women's progress in securing elected political offices increased participation in overall citizens' movements. I argue that it is not one factor alone but several, developing collectively, that have resulted in the gradual progress of women's political representation and empowerment. Drawing from South Korea's democratization process, specifically the strength of the women's movement, the institution of electoral gender quotas, and the successful execution of policies and programs, this thesis hypothesizes that women's political empowerment is progressing and will continue to do so due to societal demands.

E.   RESEARCH DESIGN

This study draws primarily from secondary sources including books, scholarly articles, political commentary, and think tank reports dealing with women's progress in South Korea since the 1980s. This period is the most relevant for measuring women's political progress, as "although the women's movement in Korea began during the early 1900s, it was not until the 1980s that women's political participation was strengthened along with mass movement for democratization."[79] Although South Korea's changes are not significant when compared to other countries, they do show South Korea's progress and future potential.

Chapter II describes women's participation in the assembly, the country's first elected female president, the progress of the women's movement, and policy changes to better illustrate the current status of women's political empowerment in South Korea. By providing details on women's participation in politics, both in terms of current absolute levels and in terms of change over time, I will argue that Korea is progressing significantly better than indicated through conventional gender-related indices. In Chapter III, the research will evaluate and explain the aforementioned patterns and outcomes of political empowerment in South Korea.

---

[79] Air-Rie Lee and Mikyung Chin, "The Women's Movement in South Korea," *Social Science Quarterly* 88, no. 5 (2007), 1209.

II. BETTER MEASURES OF WOMEN'S POLITICAL EMPOWERMENT IN SOUTH KOREA

In contrast to the picture created by conventional indices, Korean women have made noteworthy progress in the following political arenas: increasing the number of seats held in the national assembly, electing a female president, transforming civil society, and creating actual policy changes. Women's degree of political participation, in terms of advancement of over time, can paint a clearer picture of their progress toward greater political empowerment. The increase in women in the national legislature, and the voluntary appointment of women into leadership positions within political parties, the country's election of its first female president, a growing respect for the power of the female voting bloc, and public awareness and apparent approval of other potentially significant politicians, demonstrate that the glass ceiling is cracked, if not broken, with a clear path for future female electoral candidates. Lastly, the impact from policy changes and the creation of new institutions aimed at improving women's rights has the promising potential to continue these positive trends.

A. DEGREE OF PARTICIPATION IN POLITICS

1. Women as National-Level Legislators

The minority status of women in politics is deeply rooted. Korea had only forty-two women legislators between the 1st and the 13th general elections, from 1948 to 1988.[80] But this number has continued to grow since democratization. The average rate of women's participation since the establishment of the National Assembly had been below three percent, but by the 16th election in 2000, it rose to 5.9 percent.[81] More impressively, after the implementation of the reformed gender quota and proportional representation during the 17th election in 2004, it increased to over seven percent.[82]

In the latest election, in 2012, the election rate for women rose even more, quickly doubling to 15.7 percent, with women occupying 47 seats. In addition to the Political Party Act,

---

[80] Soh, "Sexual Equality, Male Superiority, and Korean Women in Politics," 75–76.
[81] Shin, "Women's Sustainable Representation and the Spillover Effect," 80–81.
[82] Ibid.

the National Assembly created the Women's Development Act, which provided a solid basis for women's participation in policymaking roles.[83] The trend of women's elections in the national assembly provides an indication that this will continue into the future. The presidential election "highlighted the importance of women as a voting bloc in South Korea's electoral politics," as the candidates pursued "the female vote with a host of policies including improved child care, reduced education costs, increased social insurance, and expanded public health care."[84] Even though the party's political agenda's recognition of women's interests was designed to gain votes, the awareness and media attention the election received undoubtedly guided Korea in the direction of improved gender equality and political activism in the future.[85]

Table 4. National Assembly Election Overview[86]

Photo Removed Due to Copyright Restrictions

In the late 1990s and the early 2000s, the status of women in the Korean parliament underwent another transformation.[87] During the late 1990s, political parties began to promote a more positive view toward women and display a more contemporary image to win over female

---

[83] Hyunjoo Min, "Development of Women-related Policies and its Implications," *GSPR 2008: Perspective Overview*, Vol. 1. Seoul: Korean Women's Development Institute, 76.

[84] Emma Campbell, "The South Korean Election: A Step Forward for Women," *East Asia Forum* (blog), 13 December 2012, http://www.eastasiaforum.org/2012/12/13/the-south-korean-election-a-step-forward-for-women/.

[85] Ibid.

[86] "19th National Assembly Election Overview Report," Republic of Korea National Election Commission, 352–353, http://www.nec.go.kr/search/search.jsp.

[87] Heike Hermanns, "Women in South Korean Politics: A Long Road to Equality," *Journal of Multidisciplinary International Studies* 3, no. 2 (2006): 3.

voters.[88] By the early 2000s, political parties concentrated on efforts to project a modern image and integrated women in their personnel line-ups, including designations of female speakers for all three main parties.[89] The main opposition party, the Grand National Party, took this one step further and elected a woman, Park Geun-hye, as the party's president.[90] Designating these women to fill these positions was significant because this was the first time in which the selections were voluntary, unlike the assembly's reactions to gender quotas.[91] Korean women have now held prestigious places in politics: president, prime minister, chairpersons of policy committee and parties. These accomplishments represent an increase not only in the quantity of women in politics, but also an increase in the degree and quality of their influence. These gradual, qualitative signs of progress should be seen as at least a partial counter to quantitative measures' depiction of minuscule progress for women's political empowerment.

Changing attitudes and behavior toward the empowerment of women takes work, but Korea is beginning to slowly understand and appreciate the importance of women's political contributions. In addition to the first elected president, other women are taking center political stage. Female legislators are beginning to attract public interest and gain political power and prestige in the legislation. As such, both the national assembly and voters have been generally more receptive to women in high political positions. In addition, female politicians are able to use unique feminine (and maternal) characteristics to their advantage. For example, a member of the conservative Saenuri Party, Na Kyung-won, a former judge, officially announced her candidacy for Seoul Mayor with the statement: "If Seoul citizens choose me, I will bring a magnificent change to Seoul in an attentive and soft manner."[92] Instead of competing with her opponents in a traditional way, she capitalized on her motherly characteristics to appeal to wider voter constituents. Na, whose daughter has Down syndrome, began her political life in 2004 to

---

[88] Ibid., 10.

[89] Ibid., 12.

[90] "Park Geun-hye," Biography.com, accessed 6 June 2014, http://www.biography.com/#!/people/park-geun-hye-21145475#thrust-into-politics&.

[91] Hermanns, "Women in South Korean Politics: A Long Road to Equality," 12.

[92] Tae-hoon Lee, "Na Joins Mayoral Race," *The Korea Times*, 23 September 2011, http://www.koreatimes.co.kr/www/news/nation/2011/09/116_95352.html.

improve the quality of life and education for intellectually challenged children.[93] She claimed victory against Justice Party's Roh Hoe-chan by a difference of 929 votes in the 2014 legislative election.[94] Her comeback victory in a legislative by-election was highly publicized, especially after she gained popularity during her campaign for Mayor of Seoul in 2011, which election she lost.[95] Congresswoman Na's political observers predict her election and return to the National Assembly will strengthen her potential for a future presidential bid.[96] Congresswomen Na is serving her third term representing the Seoul Metropolitan district and is part of two special committees—Budget and Accounts and Foreign Affairs and Unification.[97]

In addition, South Korea's main political parties have attempted to appeal to a wide range of people, especially younger voters, and to demonstrate reform credentials through the selection of more female candidates. One of the most intriguing nominations is from the ruling New Frontier Party (NPT), which selected a 27-year-old, Son Su-jo, to run against the main opposition Democratic United Party in Busan (the country's second largest city) in the 2012 elections for one of the 300 available parliamentary seats.[98] Her nomination is a sign not only that women are competing for political seats, but also that parties are attempting to appeal to younger voters and push for reforms away from the existing patriarchal system. "Son's nomination is a result of party chairwoman Park Geun-hye's pledge that the New Frontier Party will reserve some nominations for young, talented political newcomers."[99] Despite Son's loss in 2012, social media has often referred to her as a "mini-Park" and as being groomed by the party as a future successor. To be sure, Son's nomination also results from the party's attempt to attract

---

[93] Kyong-Ae Choi, "Na Hopes Special Olympics Change Views on Disabled," *The Wall Street Journal Asia* (blog), last modified 23 January 2013, http://blogs.wsj.com/korearealtime/2013/01/23/na-hopes-special-olympics-change-views-on-disabled/.

[94] Kin-Kyu Kang, "Saenuri Achieving Landslide Victory," *Korea Joongang Daily*, 31 July 2014, http://koreajoongangdaily.joins.com/news/article/Article.aspx?aid=2992809.

[95] Tae-hoon Lee, "Na Joins Mayoral Race," *The Korea Times*, 23 September 2011, http://www.koreatimes.co.kr/www/news/nation/2011/09/116_95352.html.

[96] Kin-Kyu Kang, "Saenuri Achieving Landslide Victory," *Korea Joongang Daily*, 31 July 2014, http://koreajoongangdaily.joins.com/news/article/Article.aspx?aid=2992809.

[97] The National Assembly of the Republic of Korea: Members, accessed 20 February 2015, http://korea.assembly.go.kr/mem/mem_01.jsp#Alphabet05.

[98] In-soo Nam, "In Busan, David Takes on Goliath," *The Wall Street Journal Asia* (blog), March 7, 2012, http://blogs.wsj.com/korearealtime/2012/03/07/in-busan-david-takes-on-goliath/.

[99] Ibid.

younger voters; part of the strategy is to have younger candidates. Son represents this "young" strategy -- but the fact that she is a woman is also significant. That a "youth movement" would involve a strong presence by women as well as men is not necessarily something to take for granted in South Korea. With the political glass ceiling broken by Park, future prospects for female politicians like Na and Son seem bright.

2. The Presidency

In a March 2011 survey conducted by the office of a Korean legislator, more than 60 percent of respondents said that they wanted to see more female lawmakers. In the same survey, 36.9 percent said they viewed the idea of a female president as preferable, while 36.9 percent stated that gender did not matter.[100] This survey reflected the readiness of the South Korean population for female political representation. This apparent change in public sentiment toward women's political roles represented by the survey seems to have been accurate, as South Korea elected its first female president 2 years later in 2013.

Of course, factors other than Park's gender may have had a great deal to do with her election. Some voters might have preferred President Park simply because she was the nominee of the main conservative party and because they preferred the prospect of a President Park over a left-wing president. Also, as Campbell indicates, critics argued that the first female president's "political support [was] drawn not from her own achievement but from the legacy of her father."[101] Furthermore, Bach highlights the society's view that "Park, even though she may be the first women to take the country's highest office, is in many ways exactly the wrong person to represent women's rights" because she never married nor had a family of her own.[102] This argument could result from the Confucius teaching of identifying a woman by her societal roles such as a mother, a wife, or a daughter. As a result, some were skeptical in her ability to champion women's rights because she did not know what "real" women's issues and interests were.

---

[100] Kyung-ho Kim, "Time to Shatter Political Glass Ceiling?," *The Korea Herald*, Oct 12, 2011, http://www.koreaherald.com/view.php?ud=20111011000690.

[101] Trevor Bach, "South Korea's First Female President Unlikely to Address Women's Issues," *Global Post Blogs*, April 9, 2013, http://www.globalpost.com/dispatches/globalpost-blogs/rights/south-korea-first-female-president-womens-issues-park-geun-hye.

[102] Ibid.

But Park's supporters and supporters of Korean women's political empowerment also welcomed her election as a sign of progress. And despite the criticism she has confronted, the new South Korean leader has promised to give a new face to female political figures in her country. After assuming power in February 2013, "Park has fueled a creative economy policy strengthening trade ties with the United States and China, and handled the pressure and the change of power in North Korea and a strong posture on the issue of Korean women's abuse during World War II."[103] *TIME* listed Park as one of 100 most influential people in the world, and the Prime Minister of Thailand praised "Madame Park Geun-hye [as] an inspiration for all women trying to break through the glass ceiling and for all individuals committed to serving the people."[104] *Forbes* named Park as the 11th most powerful woman in the world for 2014.[105] As such, regardless of how or why she was elected, President Park has made, and is continuing to make, strides within Korean society and in women's political empowerment. Park, as woman who achieved South Korea's highest political position, will likely serve as a precedent for women's political participation and facilitate positive changes toward gender equality and women's political empowerment in Korean society.

B. POLICY IMPROVEMENTS

Korean women's politics is truly evolving in policy terms as well; the women's political empowerment narrative is showing tangible progress.

South Korea is fairly new to a "normal democratic political life."[106] According to Darcy, "The [Korean] society is strongly committed to making a success of democracy, including establishing an equitable place for women."[107] The nation's mass media and schools stress democratic values and the need to provide equal opportunity for women.[108] "Gender equality,

---

[103] Gabriel Nieto, "Powerful Women Renovate Asian Women's Role," *ALAS Asia*, last modified December 17, 2014, http://www.alasasia.com/english/articulos.php.

[104] Yingluck Shinawatra, "Leaders: Park Geun-hye," *Time*, April 18, 2013, http://time100.time.com/2013/04/18/time-100/slide/park-geun-hye/.

[105] Caroline Howard, "The World's Most Powerful Women 2014," *Forbes*, May 28, 2014, http://www.forbes.com/profile/park-geun-hye/.

[106] R. Darcy, "Women in Politics: Korea's Progress," *Woodrow Wilson International Center for Scholars: Asia Program Special Report*, no. 132 (September 2006): 34.

[107] Ibid.

[108] Ibid.

the proclaimed goal of women's policies in Korea, is clearly expressed in the government's policies on women and it is the major agenda of the women's movement."[109] Table 5 displays women's movement issues and concerns and their impact on governmental and institutional changes from the 1980s to the 2000s.

Table 5.   Women's Movement and Political Impact[110]

Photo Removed Due to Copyright Restrictions

---

[109] Kyounghee Kim, "A Frame Analysis of Women's Policies of Korean Government and Women's Movement in the 1980s and 1990s," *Contemporary South Korean Society: A Critical Perspective,* ed. Hee-Yoeon Cho et al., (Abingdon, Oxon: Routledge, 2013), 107.

[110] Ta-young Song et al., *Saero Ssŭnŭn Yŏsŏng Pokchiron: Chaengchŏm Kwa Silch'ŏn*, trans. Sila Pang (Kyŏnggi-do P'aju-si: Yangsŏwŏn, 2011), 120–129.

Photo Removed Due to Copyright Restrictions

Korean institutions have also focused heavily on changes in the labor market to support women's labor force involvement and to foster women's empowerment.[111] The government's actions complemented the argument that "the state and state policies play a major role in shaping women's experience of paid work, politics, and family life."[112] Accordingly, the Korean Government encouraged the empowerment of economic independence via small business entrepreneurship programs such as the Business Startup Subsidy Programs for Women Engineers

---

[111] Inchoon Kim, "Developments and Characteristics of Gender Politics in South Korea: A Comparative Perspective," *Korea Observer* 43, no 4 (Winter 2012), 562.

[112] Ibid., 557.

and for Women Household heads.[113] Supported by the MOGEF and the Women's Development Fund, these programs still provide women with technical skills or women who are household heads with the ability to start a business; the programs are geared toward economically empowering low-income women to enhance their self-capacity on the path to economic independence.[114]

C. INSTITUTIONAL CHANGES

In addition to policies, institutional changes aimed at improving women's rights and interests increased, with the aim of enhancing safety and promoting the political status of women. The women's movement's strong demand for improvements has made politicians more responsive to their interests. In 1983, under the Prime Minister's office, the government established one of the first funded women's research think-tanks to provide comprehensive solutions to issues to common South Korean women's issues to foster a for a more egalitarian society.[115]

During the center-left administration of President Kim Dae Jung's (beginning in 1998), women's organizations and the government further strengthened their political cooperation by creating a new framework of government institutions.[116] President Kim created "the President's Special Committee on Women's Affairs and a position in charge of gender policy was added to each of six ministries (Labor, Education, Law, Health and Welfare, Agriculture and Forestry, and Administration and Local-Government)."[117] Gender specialists filled these newly established positions; most were women with degrees in women's studies or women's movement

---

[113] National Voluntary Presentations: Republic of Korea" in *Achieving Gender Equality, Women's Empowerment and Strengthening Development Cooperation: Dialogues at the Economic and Social Council*, prepared by the Office of ECOSOC Support Coordination, Department of Economic and Social Affairs of the United Nations (NY: United Nations, 2010), 98.

[114] "National Voluntary Presentations: Republic of Korea" in *Achieving Gender Equality, Women's Empowerment and Strengthening Development Cooperation: Dialogues at the Economic and Social Council*, prepared by the Office of ECOSOC Support Coordination, Department of Economic and Social Affairs of the United Nations (NY: United Nations, 2010), 98.

[115] "About KDWI," *Korean Women's Development Institute*, accessed 10 February 2014, http://eng.kwdi.re.kr/about/page.do?cg=history.

[116] Seung-Kyung Kim and Kyounghee Kim, "Gender Mainstreaming and the Institutionalization of the Women's Movement in South Korea," *Women's Studies International Forum* 35, no. 5 (September/October 2011), 392.

[117] Ibid.

activists.[118] In 2001, the government reorganized the Special Committee and elevated it to the cabinet level as the Ministry of Gender Equality, and since has changed its name to the Ministry of Gender Equality and Family (MOGEF).[119] The newly created ministry had three main objectives: (1) to bring about a society with gender equality, (2) to increase women's participation in society, and (3) to improve women's welfare.[120] The creation of MOGEF also enhanced other institutions' ability to support collaborations between women's associations and the state.

The MOGEF focuses its efforts on encouraging adoption of a "gender mainstreaming perspective" in building and evaluating governmental policies, including gender-based analyses and gender sensitive budgets.[121] A "gender impact assessment," as referred to in the Framework Act on Women's Development, amended on Dec 11, 2002, is a policy analysis tool to facilitate formulation and implementation of gender-equality policy, which the government can apply to the business of national finance.[122] According to MOGEF, the 2004 gender impact assessment reviewed 10 key policies for gender discrimination; this assessment expanded to 290 institutions in 2008.[123] Through this process of critique, the government attempts to create more gender-sensitive policies and further promote gender equality in society.

Furthermore, after the inauguration of the first female president – a conservative – in 2013, "The Korean government included maximizing the impact of women and closing the gender gap in its key national policy agenda."[124] The MOGEF has strengthened its coordinating role in women's policy-making to execute its vision for "a society where all family members are

---

[118] Ibid.

[119] Ibid.

[120] Kim and Kim, "Gender Mainstreaming and the Institutionalization of the Women's Movement in South Korea," 392.

[121] Min, "Development of Women-related Policies and its Implications for Future Policies Agenda in Korea," 75.

[122] "Gender Sensitive Policy," Ministry of Gender Equality & Family, Republic of Korea, last modified October 6, 2014, https://english.mogef.go.kr/sub02/sub02_10.jsp.

[123] Min, "Development of Women-related Policies and its Implications for Future Policies Agenda in Korea," 75.

[124] Yoon-Sun Cho, "How Korea's Government is Tackling the Gender Gap," *World Economic Forum Agenda*. 5 June 2014, accessed 5 June 2014, Https://agenda.weforum.org/2014/03/koreas-government-tackling-gender-gap/.

happy" and to build "an equal society sharing together."[125] Through close cooperation with relevant ministries, they expanded the number of in-house childcare facilities in the workplace.[126] The government has also established and funded the Korean Women's Development Institute (KWDI), a women's think tank. According to KWDI, "Korean women's policies consist of two types of gender issues in general: the first issue is about improvement in women's rights and interests. The second issue is related to adoption of a gender mainstreaming perspective for analyzing [the] political and social agenda."[127]

D. SUMMARY

Korean women have made significant political progress in the national legislature, the presidency, and policy. Some noteworthy elements of progress from the political sector include the steady increase in seats occupied by women in the National Assembly, the recent election of the country's first female president, and various political parties' realization of the female voting bloc's importance. Furthermore, women's societal status improved significantly in many social sectors such as in legal rights, education, and other areas. In civil society, women's role as the head of household is on the rise. Additionally, the impact from policy changes and the creation of new institutions aimed at improving women's rights have promising potential for continuing these positive trends. Thus, women's status in Korea suggests a positive trajectory toward improving women's rights and enhancing political empowerment. This degree of success in paints a more optimistic picture of women's empowerment than suggested by the GGI.

---

[125] "Vision & Emblem," About MOGEF, Ministry of Gender Equality & Family Republic of Korea, http://english.mogef.go.kr/sub01/sub01_11.jsp.

[126] Cho, "How Korea's Government Is Tackling the Gender Gap," accessed 5 June 2014.

[127] Min, "Development of Women-related Policies and its Implications for Future Policies Agenda in Korea," 74.

THIS PAGE INTENTIONALLY LEFT BLANK

III. EXPLANATION FOR THE PATTERNS AND POSSIBLE OUTCOMES

These optimistic changes in the political arena are driven by an inter-related set of factors. Urbanization and industrialization have led to an increase in education and political efficacy levels. This has driven change both directly and indirectly through its promotion of a women's movement, which itself has heled fuel concrete political and policy changes. In addition, these internal developments have been complemented by international pressure.

One portrait of a woman, Shin Saim-dang, on the new Korean bill illustrates a pattern to Korean women's empowerment: that progress is not always immense but changes are occurring. In 2009, the Bank of Korea debuted the new 50,000-won bill, the nation's highest-denomination banknote since 1973.[128] The 50,000-won bill was also significant in that it was the first time a women's portrait and her artwork appeared on a banknote in South Korea. Yet, the portrait of Shin sparked controversy and divergent views because, "while some applauded the move as an equal rights gesture in a country where men control nearly every facet of society, others [argued that] choosing Shin reinforce[d] sexist stereotypes about women's roles."[129] Over 500 years, Shin was viewed as a role model of material devotion and filial piety: she was the mother of Yi Yulgok, one of the most respected Confucian scholars in the 16th century.[130] Shin's selection also highlighted her accomplishments as a renowned female writer and calligraphist during the Joseon Kingdom, and her more recent societal fame as the "Eojin Eomeoni," or "wise mother."[131] According to the *Korea Times*, "Shin's appearance on the bill has clear implications about the improved status of women and gender equality in modern days."[132] Despite the argument that Shin might not be the role model of the "new" Korean woman in the 21st century, her portrait is a visual sign of the advancement occurring in women's status of Korea.

---

[128] "Debut of 50,000-Won Bill: Authorities Should Try to Minimize Side Effects," *Korea Times*, accessed 3 February 2015, http://www.koreatimes.co.kr/www/common/printpreview.asp?categoryCode=202&newsIdx=47257.

[129] John M. Glionna, "Women's Picture will Appear on South Korean Bank Note," *Los Angeles Times*, January 28, 2009, http://articles.latimes.com/2009/jan/28/world/fg-korea-currency28.

[130] Ibid.

[131] Ibid.

[132] Ibid.

A. INDUSTRIALIZATION, URBANIZATION, AND SOCIOECONOMIC CHANGE

Urbanization and industrialization have led to advancement in women's societal status along with an increase in education and employment levels. This socioeconomic change has also contributed to a strong women's movement.

The transformation of Korean women's status began amid the process of rapid industrialization and urbanization facilitating workforce participation and higher education. Beginning in the mid-1970s, South Korea transformed from an under-developed, agrarian economy to an industrialized, export-led nation.[133] As a result, Korea attained a remarkable growth rate of seven percent per year in real per capita income in the 25 years from 1975 to 2000.[134] For this tenacious development and economic increase, the Republic of Korea was recognized as a "miracle economy."[135] With the expansion of the economy, the need for a highly trained workforce also increased. "The full-fledged national movement for modernization required the massive participation of a female workforce, and thus women became—perhaps unintentionally—major contributors to national development."[136]

Table 6. Economically Active Population by Sex[137]

Photo Removed Due to Copyright Restrictions

---

[133] Aie-Rie Lee, "Consistency or Change in Women's Politicization in South Korea," *Policy Studies Journal* 24, no. 2 (1996): 183.

[134] Gary S. Fields and Gyeongjoon Yoo, "Falling Labor Income Inequality in Korea's Economic Growth: Patterns and Underlying Causes," *Review of Income and Wealth* 46, no. 2 (2000): 139.

[135] Ibid.

[136] Lee, "Consistency or Change in Women's Politicization in South Korea," 183.

[137] Jae-seon Joo, "Statistical Analysis of Changes in the Status of South Korean Women," *GSPR 2013* Vol. 6, 168. http://eng.kwdi.re.kr/gspr/view.do?idx=8.

Some maintain that Korea's "miracle economy" has reached its full potential. According to Ward, "Economic analysts argue that under-representation of women is holding back the South Korean economy, by failing to exploit half of the country's talent."[138] Women's participation is arguably an underexploited resource that could propel future economic growth: this is both a sign of insufficient progress and, if prior momentum is taken into account, perhaps also a sign of latent economic pressure that may be brought to bear with an ultimately positive effect on women's labor force participation. Table 4 outlines the difference between men and women in Korea's total workforce from 1980 to 2012. Women's low workforce rate remained static after 1990 and similar to what it was in 1980. This continued in 2013, at just 56 percent of working-age women participate in the workforce, which had led to "increasingly urgent problems in the world's fastest-aging developed country, where the working-age population is set to decline from next year."[139] Furthermore, *The Economist* reports in 2013 that Korea's Glass Ceiling Index score[140] was the lowest among 26 Organization for Economic Cooperation and Development countries, indicating the under-utilization of women and their limited promotion opportunities.[141]

However, this problem of low female representation in high positions can be remedied through institutional improvements. According to Reuters reporter Christine Kim, "A shortage of dependable childcare is derailing the careers of hundreds of thousands of women in South Korea."[142] Women in their twenties outnumber men in the same age group in their labor force participation rate.[143] Yet, the measurement for women in their *thirties* presents a different

---

[138] Andrew Ward, "Progress for Women Against Korean Male Domination: Appointment of First Women in Society," *Financial Times* (London edition), 13 Jul 2002, ProQuest 249254548.

[139] Christine Kim, "In South Korea, Childcare Burden Derails Women's Career," *Reuters*, January 27, 2015, http://www.reuters.com/article/2015/01/27/us-southkorea-women-childcare-idUSKBN0L00B220150127.

[140] "*The Economist* has compiled its own "glass-ceiling index" to show where women have the best chance of equal treatment at work. Based on data mainly from the OECD, it compares five indicators across 26 countries: the number of men and women respectively with tertiary education; female labor-force participation; the male-female wage gap; the proportion of women in senior jobs; and net child-care costs relative to the average wage. The first four are given equal weighting, the fifth a lower one, since not all working women have children," http://www.economist.com/blogs/graphicdetail/2013/03/daily-chart-3

[141] Ibid.

[142] Christine Kim, "In South Korea, Childcare Burden Derails Women's Career," *Reuters*, Jan 27, 2015, http://www.reuters.com/article/2015/01/27/us-southkorea-women-childcare-idUSKBN0L00B220150127.

[143] Yoon-Sun Cho, "How Korea's Government is Tackling the Gender Gap," *Forum Blog*, *World Economic Forum*, accessed 5 June 2014, http://forumblog.org/2014/03/koreas-government-tackling-gender-gap/.

picture; over 300,000 women ages 30–39 are leaving the workforce due to newly found motherhood duties and family commitments.[144] The government has realized the close relationship between future economic growth and keeping women in the workplace and has reacted to attempt to mitigate the issue. Through close cooperation with relevant ministries, they expanded the number of in-house childcare facilities in the workplace.[145] Furthermore, President Park recently announced the "three-year Economic Innovation Plan" with goals to expand the number of jobs for women from 290,000 to 1.5 million, and to increase women's employment rate from 53.9 percent to 61.9 percent.[146] Although it is too early to predict the outcome of increased childcare facilities and expansion of more jobs for women, Korea is evolving to sustain its "miracle economy."

The progress in Korea is being recognized internationally. In 2012, McKinsey & Company, a global management-consulting firm, included Korea's drive for progress in their analysis of women's representation in Asian top management. According to the research, "While deep-rooted cultural biases against working women still prevail in South Korean society, there are signs of improvement in terms of labor participation and college enrollment."[147] The research recognized the government's effort to push measures to create and sustain jobs for working mothers and concluded, "The impact has yet to be fully realized as South Korea has one of the lowest levels of female representation in senior roles, but the majority of executives are optimistic about their future—a rare finding in Asia."[148]

---

[144] Ibid.

[145] Ibid.

[146] Ibid.

[147] C. Süssmuth-Dyckerhoff, J. Wang, and J. Chen, "Women Matter: An Asian Perspective," *Australia: McKinsey & Company* (2012), 15.

[148] Ibid.

The industrialization and urbanization period also vitalized women's level of education. With the improvement in the economy, more families could support advanced education for their children, including their daughters. In 2012, women made up half the number of those holding bachelor's and master's degrees.[149] Likewise, the past 30 years of observation suggests that this trend will continue, even if not as rapidly. The rate of women attending high school quadrupled from 24 percent in 1970 to 85 percent in 1990, and women's attendance at institutions of higher education jumped from 4 percent to 24 percent.[150] Korean women are now amongst the highest educated in the world.

Furthermore, women's role in society is changing in more ways than just their status in employment and education. For instance, "The parliament's decision [in 2004] to abolish the male-oriented family registration system was an inevitable (if belated) response to the change in the times."[151] The revision of the Family Law established in 1948 guaranteed unprecedented rights for women in areas of marriage, divorce, child custody, and property inheritance.[152] The patriarchal household-head system and family law had been the backbone of Korean society and the Korean family system. The number of women household heads, who have the responsibility to support the members of the household, has increased by 3.2 times from 1980 to 2008.[153] More striking, "The increase[d] rate of women heads of household was far higher than that of men, albeit the number of men household has increased only about 1.9 times" in the same time frame.[154] Thus, updating this law and abolishing the family-head system was a fundamental change in Korean society.

---

[149] Joo, "Statistical Analysis of Changes in the Status of South Korean Women," 168.

[150] Ibid.

[151] Rosa Kim, "Legacy of Institutionalized Gender Inequality in South Korea: The Family Law," *Boston College Third World Law Journal* 14, (1994): 145.

[152] Kim, "Legacy of Institutionalized Gender Inequality in South Korea: The Family Law," 145.

[153] Joo, "Observing Changes in the status of Korean Women through Statistics," 79.

[154] Ibid.

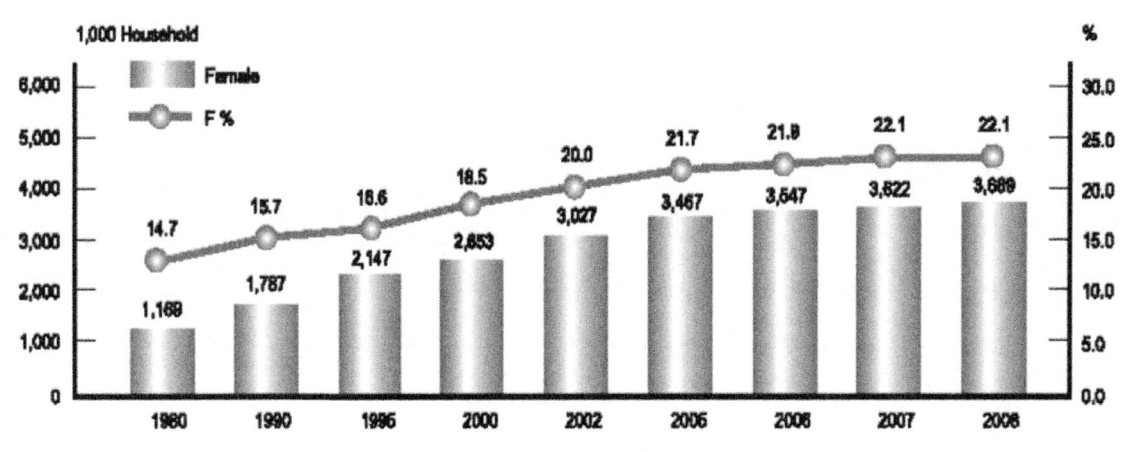

Figure 2. Female Heads of Households

Photo Removed Due to Copyright Restrictions

Figure 3. Proportion of Women with Bachelor Degrees or Higher[155]

B. CIVIL SOCIETY AND THE WOMEN'S MOVEMENT

Increasing participation by Korean women in society and higher education has produced significant changes in their basic status, outlook, and expectations. According to the United Nations' Department of Economic and Social Affairs, "In the area of gender equality and the empowerment of women, it is well known that civil society has an important role in mobilizing resources, developing new practices and working in conjunction with multiple stakeholders to

---

[155] Joo, "Statistical Analysis of Changes in the Status of South Korean Women," 168.

support the achievement of the gender-related goals."[156] Nineteenth century scholar Alexis De Tocqueville argued that civic associations pull together people with common interests and allow for self-governance on a small scale.[157] Further, "the more the number of these minor communal matters increases, the more men...acquire, even unknowingly, the capacity to pursue major ones in common."[158] As such, when opportunities for self-governance are combined with pursuit of common interests and values, civic associations can transform themselves into political organizations—groups aimed at actively shaping political outcomes.[159] Thus, the transformation of women's pursuit of political empowerment was not based only on structural change but also on "intentional collective struggle."[160] In the 1970s, South Korean women began to raise consciousness and participate in various social movements through their role as mothers and wives. Catalyzed by this social and economic participation, women began to organize and advocate for their own interests. By late 1980s, the women's movement transitioned to mainstream political agenda with a more streamlined and unified objectives, and less political antagonism.

The early experiences of Korean women's involvement in social movements revolved around the direct connection between societal expectations of women's family responsibilities and women's lack of participation in civil society. Despite this, women were able to take advantage of their domestic roles as wife, mother, and daughters to facilitate societal recognition of their interests. Women began to take advantage of every opportunity to promote their voices by connecting societal needs with their own interests. For example, in the 1970s, Korea's male-dominated agricultural society's rising organizations "began to pay attention to women as auxiliaries to their activist husbands."[161] Taking advantage of this changing attitude, some single

---

[156] "Contribution of Non-governmental Organizations," in *Achieving Gender Equality, Women's Empowerment and Strengthening Development Cooperation: Dialogues at the Economic and Social Council*, prepared by the Office of ECOSOC Support Coordination, Department of Economic and Social Affairs of the United Nations (NY: United Nations, 2010), 98.

[157] Alex de Tocqueville, *Democracy in America*, New York: Penguin Classics, 2003, 604.

[158] Ibid.

[159] De Tocqueville, *Democracy in America*, 604.

[160] Seungsook Moon, "Betwixt and Between Law and Practices: South Korean Women in the Workplace," *Woodrow Wilson International Center for Scholars: Asia Program Special Report*, no. 132 (September 2006): 6.

[161] Ibid., 479.

women also became actively involved in these organizations. By the late 1980s, women peasants organized their own autonomous movement. Similarly, in the labor sector, a movement of young female factory workers supported by student activists and Christian ministers emerged. Their demand for unpaid back wages and higher pay "came to stand as [a] symbolic beacon for labor movements" during the repression of President Park Chung Hee's authoritarian regime.[162]

With employment and higher education, the Korean women's movement furthered the opportunity to form an identity and created a catalyst for mobilization. As Lee and Chin explain, "The formation and mobilization of social movements depend on changes in resources, group organization and opportunities for collective action."[163] Through rapid growth, modernization, and higher educational opportunities, women had more job market options and advancement chances than they had in the prior period.[164] Furthermore, a greater pool of educated, middle-income women powered the movement with the required tangible resources such as money, equipment, and space.[165] The roots of Korean women's activism, in the 1980s, were "dominated by highly educated, middle-class women[;] these groups were alienated from the large population of working-class women and were not concerned with problems and interests of poor women."[166] Jeong-lim Nam lists "women's increasing participation in paid work and their direct experience of discrimination at the sex-segregated workplace" as one of the factors that contributed to the rise of the Korean middle-class women's movement at the grassroots level.[167]

Since the 1980s, autonomous women's associations have increased rapidly in number.[168] There were more than 2,000 women's organizations in 1989, compared to 23 in the 1960s and 18 in the 1970s.[169] The Korean government made an organized effort to recognize the women's

---

[162] Ibid.

[163] Aie-Rie Lee & Mikyung Chin, "The Women's Movement in South Korea," *Social Science Quarterly* 88, no. 5 (2007): 1207.

[164] Ibid., 1211–1212.

[165] Ibid.

[166] Jeong-lim Nam, "Gender Politics in the Korean Transition to Democracy," *Korean Studies* 24, no. 1 (2000): 96.

[167] Ibid., 96–97.

[168] Moon, "Civil Society and the Women's Movement in South Korea," 489.

[169] Lee & Chin, "The Women's Movement in South Korea," 1213.

movement when the legislature established the Korean Women's Development Institute (KDI) in 1983, and the President ordered the creation of the Women's Policy Review Board.[170] Although the argument that KDI was the President's "attempt to loosen up its repression of voluntary associations in response to escalating popular struggle against his military authoritarian rule," it was the catalyst that aided women's organizations in being heard in politics.[171] Additionally, in 1987, the legislature took another step with the creation of the Ministry for Women's Affairs, helping to initiate women's policy and represent different views on women's issues and promote gender equality in the government's training and educational programs.[172]

With fewer government restrictions on voluntary associations, the women's movement addressed women's limitations in the patriarchal society to their advantage and framed their issues "as the extension of women's concerns, as mothers and wives, for the well-being of their families."[173] Diversification within the women's movement indicated the growth of the movement within an expanding civil society. Additionally, the Korean women's movement began shaping legislation that promoted women's causes, "in particular, the promotion of gender equality and the empowerment of women as a social minority."[174] These organizations attempted to influence state policy by actively lobbying government officials, publicizing policy concerns, and providing policy alternatives for the state. The expansion of women's participation in civil society, accompanied by their impact on social reforms, helped transform their role beyond the restrictions set by the Confucian thinking.

One example of women's organizations' enabling women's equal representation is Korea Women's Associations United (KWAU). In February 1987, 21 progressive women's organizations came together to form the KWAU.[175] The KWAU played a central role in vocalizing the core objective of gender equality, as well as "the specific needs and interests of

---

[170] Jungia Lee, "Women's Political Representation in South Korea: Structural Responses," *Korea Observer* 22, (1991): 546.

[171] Moon, "Civil Society and the Women's Movement in South Korea," 489.

[172] Lee, "Women's Political Representation in South Korea: Structural Responses," 546–547.

[173] Moon, "Civil Society and the Women's Movement in South Korea," 490.

[174] Seungsook Moon, "Betwixt and Between Law and Practices: South Korean Women in the Workplace," *Woodrow Wilson International Center for Scholars: Asia Program Special Report*, no. 132 (September 2006): 6.

[175] Ibid.

such diverse groups of women as factory workers, clerical workers, urban housewives, rural women, and the urban poor."[176] "In the context of procedural democracy, the women's movement led by the KWAU ha[s] been involved in the institutionalized political process to legislate and revise law fundamental to the promotion of gender equality and women's empowerment."[177] "The women's movement's politics of engagement resulted in two important outcomes: first the creation of various governmental organizations responsible for gender policy; and, second, the increased participation of women's movement leaders and feminist scholars in the government and in Congress."[178]

To summarize the importance of KWAU, "the existence of the KWAU symbolized women's entry into growing civil society."[179] Reflecting general trends in the civil society of the 1990s, negotiation replaced previous antagonism between dissident women's associations and the state and replaced the dominance that the state wielded over the organizations. Despite being founded as an oppositional group working outside of the state, in 1995, KWAU registered and collaborated with the state.[180]

The new relationship between the state and the women's movement is visible in two ways. First, the state began to provide some financial support for women's associations by legislating the Women's Development Basic law in 1995. Prior to this change, the state had financed only approved organizations in order to exercise tight control over them. In contrast, the Basic Law requires the central and local governments to fund projects of women's associations with the goal of promoting gender equality and women's welfare.[181] Second, the new position permitted women's organization to take advantage of their status as a part of the state's institutions for greater influence. As such, KWAU began to pay attention to political elections, so as to be able to influence the law-making and policy-making process. As a result, some KWAU activists have been elected to the National Assembly, and its sponsored candidates have

---

[176] Moon, "Civil Society and the Women's Movement in South Korea," 489.

[177] Moon, "Betwixt and Between Law and Practices: South Korean Women in the Workplace," 6.

[178] Seung-kyung Kim & Kyounghee Kim, "Gender Mainstreaming and the Institutionalization of the Women's Movement in South Korea," *Women's Studies International Forum*, 391

[179] Moon, "Civil Society and the Women's Movement in South Korea," 490.

[180] Ibid.

[181] Ibid., 491.

been elected to local assembly seats.[182] The relationship fostered extensive involvement of the coalition of diverse women's associations in legislating and reforming laws fundamental to the promotion of gender equality and women's empowerment.

This more unified women's movement used a wide range or resources such as protests, publications, conferences, and public awareness to advocate their causes. They were able to raise consciousness, promote cultural change, open dialogue and discussions on various social issues. According to Lee and Chin, "Women's groups in Korea were successful…not because they operated outside conventional forms of institutional politics, but because they chose to work with the new institutions and parties."[183] Since the new laws challenged conventional ideas about gender and sexuality in Korean society, the women's movement had to confront varying degrees of conservative resistance to legislative attempts.[184] In the 30 years from the 1980s to the 2000s, women's collective action and organizations played a leading role in addressing gender equality by vigorously publicizing women's issues through local and national mass media, drafting bills in collaboration with lawyers and academics, and lobbying politicians.[185]

With this collaboration between the state and women's organizations, the movement was able to achieve changes toward women's political empowerment. Korea established laws to protect and promote women's rights such as the Infant Care Act, The Sexual Violence Special Act, and the Domestic Violence Prevention Act, a revisitation of the Sexual Violence Act, and the Equal Employment Law.[186] Furthermore, society could easily observe the development and influence of the women's movement given the great variety of activities they undertook in support of the establishment of the above policies. While some organizations provided direct support for women, other organizations fostered awareness and enabled the development of networks for social change. For instance, the Women's Hot Line United has devoted itself to the issues of domestic and sexual violence, offering counseling and support for abused women since

---

[182] Ibid., 490.

[183] Lee and Chin, "The Women's Movement in South Korea," 1208–1209.

[184] Moon, "Civil Society and the Women's Movement in South Korea," 492.

[185] Moon, "Betwixt and Between Law and Practices: South Korean Women in the Workplace," 6.

[186] Ibid.

1983. Similarly, the Sexual Violence Counseling Center has supported victims of sexual violence since its establishment in 1991.[187]

While some organizations directly supported women's welfare and causes, other women's organizations enabled social changes and raised political consciousness, especially in camptowns. In South Korea, entertainment districts called "camptowns" sprung up around U.S. bases to cater to U.S. military members. These organizations opened dialogues and discussions in civil society to promote cultural change and protect women's safety. For example, several active members of Women Making Peace, a women's peace organization established in 1997, and Magdalena House, a shelter for women working in the sex industry, began their work on women and violence at My Sister's Place and Saewoomtuh.[188] "My Sister's Place, established in 1986 in Durebang, was the first counseling and advocacy center to address needs of camptown women and one of the first to raise violence against women as political issues."[189] All of these centers have sponsored Korean and international academicians, artists, religious activists, and members of the media, who through their interactions with prostitutes and their advocates have helped raise awareness of camptown concerns, gender relations, sexual labor, and national security. They have also helped to create a national and transnational network of activists, advocates, sex workers, and academics to address the concerns of militarism, sexual violence, human trafficking, and human rights.[190] "In addition, the counseling centers' workers and local advocates, who have seen the needs of camptowns, have forged a critical mass of individual and organizational connections that have shaped other larger civic human rights movements."[191]

Furthermore, some of these camptown-based organizations have enabled the development of networks of social activists, university students, academics, and elected officials who have gained firsthand knowledge about the social and political impact of U.S. troops' presence on local residents.[192] In general, they have helped to raise awareness of these issues

---

[187] Moon, "Civil Society and the Women's Movement in South Korea," 490.

[188] Katherine H.S. Moon, "Resurrecting Prostitutes and Overturning Treaties: Gender Politics in the 'Anti-American' Movement in South Korea," *The Journal of Asian Studies* 44, no 1 (Feb., 2007). 135.

[189] Ibid., 134.

[190] Ibid., 135.

[191] Ibid.

[192] Ibid., 135–136.

both within and outside Korea. Through volunteer opportunities, people outside of camptowns have come to learn about the living conditions, stresses, hopes and survival skills of camptown residents.[193] In sum, the camptown advocacy groups have played an important role in developing civil society and democracy.[194] First, they have recruited and trained new political leaders. Second, by serving as living classrooms for activism with respect to national security and the U.S. troop presence, the camptown groups put gender bias, violence against women, and national security on the national political map. Third, women's advocates have helped to introduce new issues, such as anti-militarism and peace activism, to Korean civil society.[195]

The women's movement continued to launch a series of campaigns focused on their issues and concerns: removal of the patriarchal family system, democratization and local self-governance, fair labor, environmental protection, fair education, arms reduction, sexual abuse, and the retrieval of Korean "comfort women's" rights following their exploitation by Japanese soldiers during World War II. Moon contends, "Although the laws that were passed frequently fell short of the bills drafted by women's associations, even this partial success is a remarkable achievement for the women's movements, especially given their short history and scarcity of human and material resources."[196]

C. INTERNATIONAL/EXTERNAL PRESSURE

Even if Korean politics could withstand internal pressure, such pressure combined with the pressures from the international community proved too strong to ignore. As Jones argues, "Given the Korean state's eagerness to improve its standing within the international community, ministries are highly attuned to the importance of being well versed in this…parlance, thus providing a common language between the state and non-state actors."[197] The women's movement capitalized on this complex relationship to leverage the need of the society with its

---

[193] Ibid., 136.

[194] Ibid.

[195] Moon, "Resurrecting Prostitutes and Overturning Treaties: Gender Politics in the 'Anti-American' Movement in South Korea," 136.

[196] Moon, "Betwixt and Between Law and Practices: South Korean Women in the Workplace," 6.

[197] Jones, Nicola Anne. *Gender and the Political Opportunities of Democratization in South Korea.* (Gordonsville, VA: Palgrave Macmillan, 2006), 63.

government. According to Jones, "Korean women's groups have also increasingly drawn upon the language of international forums, organizations, and treaties so as to capitalize on global best practices and norms to pressure the government for needed reforms."[198] According to Kim's analysis of women-related policy agendas at Korea's National Assembly, the 1980s focused on birth control and policy concerning the use of female labor; yet, no institutions established took charge of broader women's affairs.[199]

Moreover, Kim's analysis illustrates the significant impact of the UN's orientation and programs for women policy's influence in Korea. Through analysis of assembly records, she finds that "the UN project of women's development and ratification of international treaties were the two major sources of external pressure which the Korean government could not avoid."[200] In the 1980s, the UN's approach, Women in Development (WID), was designed to focus on the "role of women alienated during the course of economic development in developing countries and recognized them as a resource that can be used for economic growth."[201] "In this context, certain progress—such as the establishment of the Korean Women's Development Institute in 1985 and the amendment of the Mother and Child Health Act in 1986—was made which brought women's issues to the level of policy discourse under the agenda of women's development."[202]

Kim and Kim suggest that "the process of institutionalization of [the] Korean women's movement can be traced back to 1995 with the emergence of 'gender mainstreaming.'"[203] Gender mainstreaming is a major international strategy for women's policies and the concept was recognized in the UN's 1995 Beijing Platform for Action Forum.[204] "Mainstreaming has served as a useful discursive tool to call for the recognition of gender inequality as not just a 'women's issue,' as well as gender sensitivity analysis, gender budgeting, and gender

---

[198] Ibid.

[199] Kyounghee Kim, "A Frame Analysis of Women's Policies of Korean Government and Women's Movement in the 1980s and 1990s," n *Contemporary South Korean Society: A Critical Perspective,* ed. Hee-Yoeon Cho et al., (Abingdon, Oxon: Routledge, 2013), 109.

[200] Ibid., 112.

[201] Ibid.

[202] Ibid.

[203] Kim & Kim, "Gender Mainstreaming and Institutionalization of Women's Movement in Korea," 391.

[204] Jones, *Gender and the Political Opportunities of Democratization in South Korea,* 63.

disaggregated data collection."[205] The most critical component of gender mainstreaming in South Korea has been the collaboration between the women's movement and the government, and the consequent increase of the number of women in high-level positions, especially during the Kim Dae Jung and Roh Moo Hyun administrations (1997-2007).[206] As depicted in Figure 4, women's participation in government committees also increased during this period.

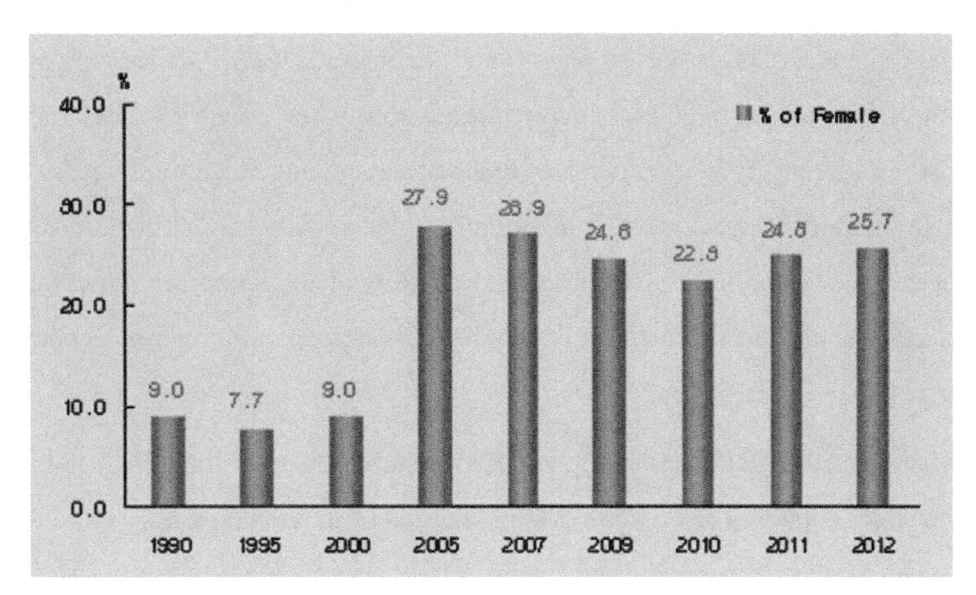

Figure 4. Women's Participation in Government Committees[207]

Scholars argue that gender quotas "are the most visible way and direct mechanism that political parties have used to increase women's parliamentary representation."[208] Others argue that they "challenge well-defined analytical frameworks and established ways to study political life."[209] The gender quota played an important role in bringing about change in a society struggling with patriarchal gender order and traditional Confucian systems. Despite the fact that "the Constitution of Korea Article II rules that all citizens are equal before the law, and there

---

[205] Ibid.

[206] Kim and Kim, "Gender Mainstreaming and Institutionalization of Women's Movement in Korea," 391.

[207] Jae-Seon Joo, Chi-Seon Song, and Geon-Pyo Park, *Statistical Handbook: Women in Korea 2013*, 68, Seoul: Korean Women's Development Institute, http://eng.kwdi.re.kr/gender/view.do?pageNo=1&idx=2031&no=8.

[208] Miki Caul, "Political Parties and the Adoption of Candidate of Gender Quotas: A Cross-National Analysis," *The Journal of Politics* 63, no. 4 (November 2001), 1214.

[209] Par Zetterberg, "The Dynamic Relationship between Gender Quotas and Political Institutions," *Politics & Gender* 9, no. 3 (2013), 316.

may be no discrimination on the basis of gender," discussion of the gender quota did not occur until United Nations' Fourth World Conference on Women in 1995.[210] The conference aided Koreans in understanding the importance of women's political representation and "spread the notion that [a] gender quota is the fastest track to achieve the goal."[211]

There exist different views on why countries adopt gender quotas. According to Ronald Inglehart and Pippa Norris' revised modernization theory, the "bundle of societal transformation that accompany[ies] economic development and democratization includes progress toward gender equality."[212] Inglehart and Norris hypothesize that when countries industrialize, women enter the work force, fertility levels decrease, female literacy and education increase, and gender attitudes begin to shift. They posit that as countries "move toward the postindustrial state of development, new social policies promote gender equality at work and in the public sphere."[213] With a rise in the women's movement in demanding those policies, tools like gender quota help initiate change.

Another plausible explanation for gender quota adoption is the world polity theory of John Meyer and colleagues. They assert, "Many features of the contemporary nation-state derive from worldwide models constructed and propagated through global cultural and associational processes."[214] The theory predicts that as a country's ties to the world polity increases, its likelihood of quota adoption should also increase, if all else is equal. These ties to the world polity is measured by the presence of international nongovernmental organizations, "which diffuse and promote human rights principles globally."[215] Sarah Bush adds, "International organizations play a key role in spreading 'policy scripts,' or models for legitimate action."[216] As a key part of international democracy promotion, the UN promoted gender equality, including

---

[210] Eunyoung Soh, "Ten Years' Experience of Gender Quota System in Korean Politics," GEMC Journal, no. 4 (2013): 99.

[211] Soh, "Ten Years' Experience of Gender Quota System in Korean Politics," 99.

[212] Sarah Sunn Bush, "International Politics and the Spread of Quotas for Women in Legislatures," *International Organization* 65, Winter 2011, 108.

[213] Ibid.

[214] Ibid.

[215] Ibid., 109.

[216] Ibid., 108

gender quotas, as an institutional improvement to help developing countries increase women's political representation.

South Korea can be seen as a supporting case for both theories. The country as a whole "did not have many arguments about the pros and cons about the gender quotas because people shared [the] consensus that women's participation in politics was extremely low" and wanted to improve this.[217] The Republic of Korea is one of the State Parties to the United Nation's Convention on the Elimination of All Forms of Discrimination against Women (CEDAW). Since joining this UN convention, "the Government of the Republic of Korea has taken definitive steps towards advancing the status of Korean women."[218] Korea exemplifies the argument that quotas can have unplanned effects, such as formal rules' turning into societal norms, "reinforcing attitudes toward women in politics."[219] According to CEDAW's 1998's fourth periodic report for South Korea, the country's progress was achieved "by focusing its gender policies on realizing an egalitarian society wherein women are respected and can participate in all realms of national life on an equal basis with men and on utilizing their capacities to the full extent."[220] Thus, the continuations of governmental efforts to promote women's rights and pursue mainstreaming gender equality have been strengthened since "once women are in position[s] of power, it may become more difficult to exclude them in the future."[221]

The gender quota system facilitated not only an increase in women's participation but also awareness of politics. As argued by scholars, "women's inclusion by candidate quotas and other temporary special measures…[is] critical to increasing the opportunities for women to gain political experience…while improving the quality of women's substantive political contributions

---

[217] Soh, "Ten Years' Experience of Gender Quota System in Korean Politics," 99.

[218] "Fourth Periodic Report: South Korea," United Nations Convention on the Elimination of All Forms of Discrimination against Women; accessed 23 February 2015, http://daccess-dds-ny.un.org/doc/UNDOC/GEN/N98/099/77/IMG/N9809977.pdf?OpenElement.

[219] Caul, "Political Parties and the Adoption of Candidate of Gender Quotas: A Cross-National Analysis," 1226.

[220] "Fourth Periodic Report: South Korea," United Nations Convention on the Elimination of All Forms of Discrimination against Women; accessed 23 February 2015, http://daccess-dds-ny.un.org/doc/UNDOC/GEN/N98/099/77/IMG/N9809977.pdf?OpenElement.

[221] Caul, "Political Parties and the Adoption of Candidate of Gender Quotas: A Cross-National Analysis," 1226.

and encouraging an inclusive political culture."[222] Women's participation in governmental committees had only reached 2.2 percent in 1984, but the rate has considerably increased since, reaching 25.7 percent in 2012.[223] Consequently, "An index to evaluate whether women are well represented in policy-making is the proportion of women in government positions."[224] By establishing and executing Women's Employment Goals (1996-2002) and Gender Equality Employment Goals (2003-2007), the government has achieved a substantial increase in women's employment in governmental positions.[225] These policies were enacted as part of the framework in the Women's Development Act. According to the Korean Ministry of Political Affairs, "the purpose of the Act is to promote gender equality and increase women's participation in all the aspects of political, economic, social and cultural fields."[226] Under this Act, Chapter III, Article 15, "The State and local governments shall devise the measures to expand women's participation in the procedure of policy decision of various committees."[227] Gender quotas supported the fulfillment of this policy. Although gender quotas may not solve gender disparity issues as a whole, in South Korea, they have empowered women to seek political participation and thereby become more integral parts of society.

Korea's gender quotas were first introduced just before the 2000 national election in the Law on Political Parties.[228] "Article 47 of the Public Official Election Act specifies that for the list of proportional representation elections whereby 56 deputies are elected, political parties must include 50 percent women on candidate lists."[229] For the election, whereby 243 representatives are elected in single-member districts, this law encouraged 30 percent voluntary candidate quotas for women on the party's proportional representation lists; however, due to

---

[222] Jacqui True, Sara Niner, Swati Parashar, and Nicole George, "2012 Women's Political Participation in Asia and the Pacific." In *New York: SSRC Conflict Prevention and Peace Forum*, 17.

[223] Hyunjoo Min, "Development of Women-related Policies and its Implications," 76.

[224] Ibid.

[225] Ibid.

[226] "The Women's Development Act" Ministry of Political Affairs: Republic of Korea; accessed 23 February 2015, http://www.un.org/esa/gopher-data/conf/fwcw/natrep/NatActPlans/korea/korea1.

[227] Ibid.

[228] Shin, "Women's Sustainable Representation and the Spillover Effect," 82.

[229] "Global Database of Quotas for Women," *Quota Project*, last updated 4 April 2014, http://www.quotaproject.org/uid/countryview.cfm?CountryCode=KR.

non-binding requirements for compliance, political parties disregarded the recommendation.[230] It was not until 2002 and 2004 that electoral system reforms shaped more effective gender quota requirement enforcement measures.[231] Article 49 and 52 mandate that "lists of candidates that do not comply with the gender quota provisions shall be rejected."[232] Additionally, Article 26 specified that "parties that nominate female candidates for the national elections receive subsidies."[233] The average women's share of legislative seats since the establishment of the National Assembly was below 3 percent, but by the 16th election in 2000, it rose to 5.6 percent. More impressively, after the implementation of the reformed gender quota and proportional representation during the 17th election in 2004, it increased over 7 percent.[234] In the latest 2012 election, the election rate for women doubled to 15.7 percent, with 47 seats. These accomplishments resulted from opportunities set by the gender quota system and women's organization's careful strategy.

In the 2004 election, women gained a significant political representation breakthrough: an unprecedented 39 women (13 percent of total legislators) were elected.[235] Using a well-known American nongovernmental organization strategy that has played a major role in increasing American women's political representation, Korean women's organizations created their own *Emily's List*. The newly established "Women for Clean Politics Network" created a viable women candidates' list from diverse social groups' solicitations and recommendations. The candidates ranged from highly respected professionals such as lawyers, doctors, and professors to women's rights activists. The *List of 100 Women* was, in turn, presented to all political parties to serve as a database of suitable candidates. The *List of 100 Women* campaign was also publicized and gained positive support from the mainstream media; this deepened public awareness with "an emphasis on the disjuncture between Korea's high level of development and educational achievement yet low women's political

---

[230] Shin, "Women's Sustainable Representation and the Spillover Effect," 82.

[231] Shin, "Women's Sustainable Representation and the Spillover Effect," 82.

[232] Quota Project, Global Database of Quotas for Women, last updated 4 April 2014, http://www.quotaproject.org/uid/countryview.cfm?CountryCode=KR.

[233] Ibd.

[234] Shin, "Women's Sustainable Representation and the Spillover Effect," 80–81.

[235] Jones, *Gender and the Political Opportunities of Democratization in South Korea*, 187.

representation."[236] Although falling short of the target of 100 female legislators, the 2004 election presaged female political representation's future success.

Additionally, when compared to other nations that have adopted a gender quota system for national elections, Korea ranks higher than average (see Table 7). The increase in Korean women's political representation from 3 percent to 13 percent is an impressive leap, and the greatest change among countries that have adopted gender quotas. "On the Inter-Parliamentary Union evaluations, Korea ranked only 91st out of 102 countries in 1997 and had shown little improvement by 2002 (102nd of 123), but improved sharply (65th of 125) following the 2004 breakthrough."[237] Although higher women's representation does not necessarily correlate with more a gender-friendly government, the leap is significant since Korean women remain subject to strict Confucian gender roles. The gradualism of political representation accompanied by an increase of women in leadership positions shows optimism that women's political empowerment and acceptance in society are occurring. Therefore, indicators would suggest that progress for the future role of women in politics is more likely.

---

[236] Ibid.

[237] Jones, *Gender and the Political Opportunities of Democratization in South Korea*, 183.

Table 7.   Statutory Gender Quotas in Use Worldwide[238]

Photo Removed Due to Copyright Restrictions

---

[238] Pippa Norris, *Electoral Engineering: Voting Rules and Political Behavior*, New York: Cambridge University Press, 2004, 194–195.

[239] I included South Korea's information in table provided by Pippa Norris (see footnote 223).

D. SUMMARY

Along with Korea's economic development, women's socioeconomic status, education level, and societal awareness grew. Due to these significant changes in their basic status, outlook, and expectations, women began to organize and advocate collectively for their own interests. The women's movement and its successful collaboration with the government drove an increase in representation and greater power in politics. The women's movement also led to concrete political and policy changes. These changes were also fostered by the international community's influence. External pressures combined with the internal political dialogue to improve women's political status. Trends of improvement in women's rights in Korea are changing a previously androcentric society. In sum, the progressive momentum of women's political empowerment from past to present suggests strong prospects for future advancement.

IV. CONCLUSION

Mr. Ban Ki-Moon, the Secretary-General of the United Nations, stresses the importance of achieving gender equality and women's empowerment. He posits that "until women and girls are liberated from poverty and injustice, all our goals—peace, security, sustainable development—stand in jeopardy."[240] Women's political empowerment and participation open up decision-making processes and ensure the involvement of under-represented groups such as women, which strengthens and advances a democratic society. South Korea has evolved into a country where "the quantitative expansion of civil society has been accompanied by its qualitative transformation."[241] Advancements in Korean women's political empowerment have secured significant changes in policy, institutions, and participation. Yet, embedded patriarchal cultures will persist to conflict with the changing society, and create future tasks, barriers, and obstacles. Despite all the future unknowns, I have observed three generations of women's empowerment in my family. Korean women have overcome many hurdles and women's empowerment has progressed. Given the potential for further growth, I predict that my three-year-old daughter will witness even more advancements in women's status in Korean society.

A. SUMMARY OF FINDINGS

Korean women have come a long way; however, they still have a way to go in changing androcentric politics and civil society. State-led efforts to address the disparity between the genders and to guide women to pursue political participation in the national legislature have not always been successful, in part because of the deep-rooted, two-thousand-year-old culture and traditions of Confucianism.[242] However, the androcentric tendency within Korean civil society is changing. Evidence of this includes the progress enhancement of women's societal role, effective women's movement strategies, and an increase in women's political participation.

---

[240] Ki-Moon Ban, "Increasing Uniform Delivery through Collective Action," in *Achieving Gender Equality, Women's Empowerment and Strengthening Development Cooperation: Dialogues at the Economic and Social Council*, prepared by the Office of ECOSOC Support Coordination, Department of Economic and Social Affairs of the United Nations (New York: United Nations, 2010), 14.

[241] Moon, "Carving Out Space: Civil Society and Women's Movement in South Korea," 484.

[242] Chin, "Reflections on Women's Empowerment through Local Representation in South Korea," 315.

As KWDI highlights, "Korean society's process of compressive fluctuation of the family has affected an increase in segmentation and complexity between generations."[243] As such, this social imbalance causes "weakening of the foundation of social consensus toward the concept and function of family, and an objective prejudgment of the present changes and future direction of the change is ever the most important and necessary in policy planning."[244] Given the continuously changing concept of what constitutes a family with each new generation, women's role in the Korean family and society is also shifting. The Korean government also acknowledges the changing social environment and family structure:

> The family is undergoing a lot of changes in Korea. Environment scanning was used to investigate the main driving forces behind changes in the family, and the results found that these were low fertility, population aging, intensification of an unstable economy, an increase in working women, a need for improved welfare and strengthening policy and development in science and technology number of people per convergence.[245]

As a result, women's increasing influence in Korean politics is even more critical to further women's political empowerment in line with improving social conditions.

B. IMPLICATIONS

On January 11, 2015, "President Park Geun-hye participated in the new year greeting ceremony hosted by the KDWI and stated that 'in 2015, the government would focus on increasing female employment and enabling a better balance of work and family.'"[246] To craft fitting policies that address changing needs and expectations of individuals and their socio-cultural environments, the government must adapt. Through a closer examination of Korea's progress toward women's political empowerment, we can conclude that the key determinant of success lies in the collective effort of the people, the society, and the government. Furthermore, women's organizations, NGOs, and citizen's organizations have considerable power to alter both

---

[243] Hye-Kyong Chang, Chang, Eun-ji Kim, Young-ran Kim, Hye-young Kim, and Jae-hoon Chung, "The Future of Families and Future Prospects for Gender Equality and Family Policy" (*GSPR 2012* Vol. 5) (Seoul: Korean Women's Development Institute), 79, http://eng.kwdi.re.kr/gspr/view.do?idx=1.

[244] Ibid.

[245] Ibid.

[246] Korea Clickers (Korea.net) comment on Facebook, 11 January 2015, https://www.facebook.com/KoreaClickers/posts/10153018793939521.

cultural and institutional conditions to expand political empowerment for women. Thus, Korean society possesses both institutions and policymakers that can further implement policies in support of gender equality and women's empowerment.

Women in political leadership positions include the President, and changes in policies and institutions have resulted in profound outcomes in Korean society. The success rate of female candidates running for the national assembly is similar to that of male candidates. To validate whether the increase in the pool of viable women candidates will result in similar rise in the women elected to political office requires closer examination.[247] In addition, to ascertain whether President Park's election validates the recent societal improvements in Korean women's status needs further assessment.

Changes in politics and society will continue to evolve in the upcoming years. How these changes will impact this Confucius-dominated society and its sense of identity remains unknown. The difficult transition from the old, patriarchal Korea will need to be closely monitored, and further studies are required to determine whether the progressive changes women attain through political empowerment will erode the cultural and social forces that maintain South Korea's patriarchies. But if patterns up till this point are any guide, the impact of women's empowerment in South Korea will remain strong.

---

[247] Chin, "Reflections on Women's Empowerment through Local Representation in South Korea," 315

THIS PAGE INTENTIONALLY LEFT BLANK

LIST OF REFERENCES

Alsop, Ruth, Mette Bertelsen, and Jeremy Holland. *Empowerment in Practice: From Analysis to Implementation*. Washington, DC: The World Bank, 2006.

Ban, Ki-Moon. "Increasing Uniform Delivery through Collective Action." In *Achieving Gender Equality, Women's Empowerment and Strengthening Development Cooperation: Dialogues at the Economic and Social Council,* prepared by the Office of ECOSOC Support Coordination, Department of Economic and Social Affairs of the United Nations. New York: United Nations, 2010, 12–20.

Bookman, Ann, and Sandra Morgen. *Women and the Politics of Empowerment*. Philadelphia: Temple University Press, 1988.

Bush, Sarah Sunn. "International Politics and the Spread of Quotas for Women in Legislatures." *International Organization* 65 (2011): 103–137.

Caul, Miki. "Political Parties and the Adoption of Candidate Gender Quotas: A Cross–National Analysis." *The Journal of Politics* 63, no. 4 (2001): 1214–1229.

Chang, Hye-Kyong. Eun-ji Kim, Young-ran Kim, Hye-young Kim, and Jae-hoon Chung. "The Future of Families and Future Prospects for Gender Equality and Family Policy." (*GSPR 2012* Vol. 5) Seoul: Korean Women's Development Institute. http://eng.kwdi.re.kr/gspr/view.do?idx=1.

Chin, Mikyung. "Reflections on Women's Empowerment through Local Representation in South Korea." *Asian Survey* 44, no. 2 (2004): 295–315.

Cho, Yoon-Sun. "How Korea's Government is Tackling the Gender Gap," *World Economic Forum Agenda*. 5 June 2014. https://agenda.weforum.org/2014/03/koreas-government-tackling-gender-gap/.

Darcy, R. "Women in Politics: Korea's Progress," *Woodrow Wilson International Center for Scholars: Asia Program Special Report*, no. 132 (September 2006): 27–34.

Department of Economic and Social Affairs of the United Nations. "Contribution of Non-governmental Organizations." In *Achieving Gender Equality, Women's Empowerment and Strengthening Development Cooperation: Dialogues at the Economic and Social Council*, 175–186. New York: United Nations, 2010.

———. "National Voluntary Presentations: Republic of Korea." In *Achieving Gender Equality, Women's Empowerment and Strengthening Development Cooperation: Dialogues at the Economic and Social Council*, prepared by the Office of ECOSOC Support Coordination, Department of Economic and Social Affairs of the United Nations (NY: United Nations, 2010). http://www.un.org/en/ecosoc/newfunct/amrnational2010.shtml.

De Tocqueville, Alex. *Democracy in America*. New York: Penguin Classics, 2003.

Fields, Gary S., and Gyeongjoon Yoo. "Falling Labor Income Inequality in Korea's Economic Growth: Patterns and Underlying Causes," *Review of Income and Wealth* 46, no. 2 (2000): 139–159.

Fleckenstein, Timo, and Soohyun Christine Lee. "The Politics of Postindustrial Social Policy Family Policy Reforms in Britain, Germany, South Korea, and Sweden." *Comparative Political Studies* 47, no. 4 (2014): 601–630.

"Fourth Periodic Report: South Korea." United Nations Convention on the Elimination of All Forms of Discrimination against Women. Accessed 23 February 2015, http://daccess-dds-ny.un.org/doc/UNDOC/GEN/N98/099/77/IMG/N9809977.pdf?OpenElement.

Glionna, John M. "Women's Picture Will Appear on South Korean Bank Note." *Los Angeles Times*. January 28, 2009. http://articles.latimes.com/2009/jan/28/world/fg-korea-currency28.

Grown, Caren, Geeta Rao Gupta, and Aslihan Kes. *Taking Action: Achieving Gender Equality and Empowering Women*. London: Earthscan, 2005.

Hausmann, Ricardo, Saadia Zahidi, Laura Tyson, Klaus Schwab, and Laura D'Andrea Tyson. "Global Gender Gap Report 2013." The World Economic Forum. Assessed 20 May 2014. http://reports.weforum.org/global-gender-gap-report-2013.

Hermanns, Heike. "Women in South Korean Politics: A Long Road to Equality." *PORTAL Journal of Multidisciplinary International Studies* 3, no. 2 (2006).

Howard, Caroline. "The World's Most Powerful Women 2014." *Forbes*. May 28, 2014. http://www.forbes.com/profile/park-geun-hye/.

Htun, Mala. "Is Gender like Ethnicity? The Political Representation of Identity Groups." *Perspectives on Politics* 2, no. 03 (2004): 439–458.

Jones, Nicola Anne. *Gender and the Political Opportunities of Democratization in South Korea*. Gordonsville, VA: Palgrave Macmillan, 2006.

Joo, Jae-Seon, Chi-Seon Song, and Geon-Pyo Park. *Statistical Handbook: Women in Korea 2013*, 68. Seoul: Korean Women's Development Institute. http://eng.kwdi.re.kr/gender/view.do?pageNo=1&idx=2031&no=8.

Joo, Jae-seon. "Observing Changes in the status of Korean Women through Statistics." *GSPR 2008: Perspective Overview* Vol. 1. Seoul: Korean Women's Development Institute, 78–87. http://eng.kwdi.re.kr/gspr/view.do?idx=1.

Joo, Jae-seon. "Statistical Analysis of Changes in the Status of South Korean Women," *GSPR 2013*. Vol. 6. Seoul: Korean Women's Development Institute, 156–167. http://eng.kwdi.re.kr/gspr/view.do?idx=8.

Kang, Kin-Kyu. "Saenuri Achieving Landslide Victory." *Korea Joongang Daily*. July 31, 2014. http://koreajoongangdaily.joins.com/news/article/Article.aspx?aid=2992809.

Karl, Marilee. *Women and Empowerment: Participation and Decision Making*. Vol. 10. London: Zed Books, 1995.

Kim, In Choon. "Developments and Characteristics of Gender Politics in South Korea: A Comparative Perspective." *Korea Observer* 43, no 4 (Winter 2012), 557–586.

Kim, Kyunghee. "A Frame Analysis of Women's Policies of Korean Government and Women's Movement in the 1980s and 1990s." In *Contemporary South Korean Society: A Critical Perspective,* edited by Hee-Young Cho, Lawrence Surendra and Hyo-Je Cho, 107–122. Abingdon, Oxon: Routledge, 2013.

Kim, Kyung-ho. "Time to Shatter Political Glass Ceiling?" *Korea Herald*. October 12, 2011. http://www.koreaherald.com/view.php?ud=20111011000690.

Kim, Rosa. "Legacy of Institutionalized Gender Inequality in South Korea: The Family Law." *Boston College Third World Law Journal* 14 (1994): 145–162.

Kim, Seung-kyung, and Kyounghee Kim, "Gender Mainstreaming and Institutionalization of Women's Movement in Korea." In *Women's Studies International Forum* 34, no. 5 (2011): 390–400.

Koh, Eunkang. "Gender Issues and Confucian Scriptures: Is Confucianism Incompatible with Gender Equality in South Korea?" *Bulletin of the School of Oriental and African Studies* 71, no. 02 (2008): 345–362.

Korea Times. "Debut of 50,000-Won Bill: Authorities Should Try to Minimize Side Effects." *Korea Times*. Last accessed 3 February 2015. http://www.koreatimes.co.kr/www/common/printpreview.asp?categoryCode=202&newsIdx=47257.

Lee, Aie-Rie. "Consistency or Change in Women's Politicization in South Korea." *Policy Studies Journal* 24, no. 2 (1996): 183–200.

Lee, Aie-Rie, and Hyun-Chool Lee. "The Women's Movement in South Korea Revisited." *Asian Affairs: An American Review* 40, no. 2 (2013): 43–66.

Lee, Aie-Rie, and Mikyung Chin. "The Women's Movement in South Korea." *Social Science Quarterly* 88, no. 5 (2007): 1205–1226.

Lee, Jungia. "Women's Political Representation in South Korea: Structural Responses." *Korea Observer* 22 (1991): 546–547.

Lee, Tae-hoon. "Na Joins Mayoral Race." *The Korea Times*. 23 September 2011. http://www.koreatimes.co.kr/www/news/nation/2011/09/116_95352.html.

Matland, Richard E. "Structuring Representation: Women's Access to Political Power across the World." *Harvard International Review* 32, no. 1 (2010): 46–48.

Min, Hyunjoo. "Development of Women-related Policies and its Implications for Future Policies Agenda in Korea." *GSPR 2008: Perspective Overview*. Vol. 1. Seoul: Korean Women's Development Institute, 74–87. http://eng.kwdi.re.kr/gspr/view.do?idx=1.

Ministry of Gender Equality & Family, Republic of Korea. "Gender Sensitive Policy." Ministry of Gender Equality & Family, Republic of Korea, October 6, 2014, https://english.mogef.go.kr/sub02/sub02_10.jsp.

Moon, Katharine. "Resurrecting prostitutes and overturning treaties: Gender politics in the "anti-American" movement in South Korea." *The Journal of Asian Studies* 66, no. 01 (2007): 129–157.

Moon, Seungsook. "Carving Out Space: Civil Society and the Women's Movement in South Korea." *The Journal of Asian Studies* 61, no. 02 (2002): 473–500.

———. "Betwixt and Between Law and Practices: South Korean Women in the Workplace." *Woodrow Wilson International Center for Scholars: Asia Program Special Report*. No 132. September 2006.

Nam, In-soo. "In Busan, David Takes on Goliath." *The Wall Street Journal Asia* (blog). Last modified March 7, 2012. http://blogs.wsj.com/korearealtime/2012/03/07/in-busan-david-takes-on-goliath/.

———. "South Korean Women Get Even, At Least in Number." The Wall Street Journal (blog). 1 July 2013, http://blogs.wsj.com/korearealtime/2013/07/01/south-korean-females-get-even-at-least-in-number/.

Nam, Jeong-Lim. "Gender politics in the Korean transition to democracy." *Korean Studies* (2000): 94–112.

Nieto, Gabriel. "Powerful Women Renovate Asian Women's Role." *ALAS Asia*. Last modified December 17, 2014. http://www.alasasia.com/english/articulos.php.

Norris, Pippa. *Electoral Engineering: Voting Rules and Political Behavior*. New York: Cambridge University Press, 2004.

Organizational Economic Cooperation and Development. "List of OECD Member countries - Ratification of the Convention on the OECD." Accessed 10 August 2014. http://www.oecd.org/about/membersandpartners/list-oecd-member-countries.htm.

Park, Kyung. "Political representation and South Korean Women." *The Journal of Asian Studies* 58, no. 02 (1999): 432–448.

Parpart, Jane L., Shirin M. Rai, and Kathleen A. Staudt, eds. *Rethinking Empowerment: Gender and Development in a Global/Local World*, London: Routledge, 2003.

Quota Project. "Global Database of Quotas for Women." Last modified 4 April 2014. http://www.quotaproject.org/uid/countryview.cfm?CountryCode=KR.

Republic of Korea National Election. "19th National Assembly Election Overview Report.." Last accessed 1 February 2015. http://www.nec.go.kr/search/search.jsp.

Shin, Eui Hang. "The Role of NGOs in Political Elections in South Korea: The Case of the Citizens' Alliance for the 2000 General Elections." *Asian Survey* 43, no. 4 (July/August 2003), 697–715.

Shin, Ki-young. "The Politics of the Family Law Reform Movement in Contemporary Korea: A Contentious Space for Gender and the Nation," *Journal of Korean Studies* 11, no. 1 (Fall 2006), 93–125.

―――. "Women's sustainable representation and the spillover effect of electoral gender quotas in South Korea." *International Political Science Review* 35, no. 1 (2014): 80–92.

Shinawatra, Yingluck. "Leaders: Park Geun-hye." *Time*. April 18, 2013. http://time100.time.com/2013/04/18/time-100/slide/park-geun-hye/.

Soh, Chung-Hee Sarah. "Sexual Equality, Male Superiority, and Korean Women in Politics: Changing Gender Relations in a 'Patriarchal Democracy.'" *Sex Roles* 28, no. 1–2 (1993): 73–90.

Soh, Eunyoung. "Ten Years' Experience of Gender Quota System in Korean Politics," *GEMC Journal*, no. 4 (2011): 98–104.

Song, Ta-young, Mi-joo Kim, Hee-kyung Choi, and Soo-jung Jang. *Saero Ssŭnŭn Yŏsŏng Pokchiron: Chaengchŏm Kwa Silch'ŏn*. Translated by Sila Pang. Kyŏnggi-do P'aju-si: Yangsŏwŏn, 2011.

Suh, Doowon. "The Dual Strategy and Gender Policies of the Women's Movement in Korea: Family Headship System Repeal through Strategic Innovation." *Sociological Focus* 44, no. 2 (2011): 124–148.

Sung, Sirin. "Women Reconciling Paid and Unpaid Work in a Confucian Welfare State: The Case of South Korea." *Social Policy & Administration* 37, no. 4 (2003): 342–360.

Süssmuth-Dyckerhoff, C., J. Wang, and J. Chen. "Women Matter: An Asian Perspective." *McKinsey and Company* (2012).

True, Jacqui, Sara Niner, Swati Parashar, and Nicole George. "2012 Women's Political Participation in Asia and the Pacific." In *New York: SSRC Conflict Prevention and Peace Forum, 2013.*

Tuminez, Astrid S., and Vishakha N. Desai. "Power to Women in Asia: It's Time to Remove the Entrenched Social and Cultural Barriers that Prevent Women from Fulfilling Their Potential." *The Straight Time.* 19 May 2012. http://newshub.nus.edu.sg/news/1205/PDF/POWER-st-19may-pD12.pdf.

United Nations Development Programme. Human Development Reports: Gender Inequality Index. 19 August 2014. http://hdr.undp.org/en/content/table-4-gender-inequality-index.

Ward, Andrew. "Progress for Women against Korean Male Domination: Appointment of First Women in Society." *Financial Times* (London edition), 13 Jul 2002, ProQuest 249254548.

Wieringa, Saskia. "Women's Interests and Empowerment: Gender Planning Reconsidered." *Development and Change* 25, no. 4 (1994): 829–848.

World Bank, The Per Capita Income. Accessed 10 August 2014. http://data.worldbank.org/indicator/NY.GDP.PCAP.CD.

Zetterberg, Par. "The Dynamic Relationship between Gender Quotas and Political Institutions." *Politics & Gender* 9, no. 3 (2013), 316–321.

Printed in Great Britain
by Amazon